WORSHIP, FEASTING, REST, MERCY

WORSHIP, FEASTING, REST, MERCY

The Christian Sabbath

Daniel Howe

GRASSMARKET PRESS
PITTSBURGH, PENNSYLVANIA

© 2023 Daniel Howe
Grassmarket Press

an imprint of
Crown & Covenant Publications
7408 Penn Avenue
Pittsburgh, PA 15208
crownandcovenant.com
All rights reserved.

Second printing, 2024

ISBN: 978-1-943017-63-8
eBook: 978-1-943017-64-5
Library of Congress Control Number: 2023931703

Printed in the United States of America

Theological editors of Grassmarket Press: Daniel Howe and Kyle Borg.

Text font is Minion Pro set in 11/15 point. Chapter titles are Mr Eaves XL Mod Nar OT. Interior and cover design by Esther Howe. Photograph of Grassmarket Square is from the Reformed Presbyterian Church of Scotland. Used by permission.

Scripture quotations are from the ESV® Bible (The Holy Bible, English Standard Version®), copyright © 2001 by Crossway, a publishing ministry of Good News Publishers. Used by permission. All rights reserved. The ESV text may not be quoted in any publication made available to the public by a Creative Commons license. The ESV may not be translated into any other language.

All rights reserved. No part of this book may be reproduced or stored in a retrieval system in any form by any means (electronic, mechanical, photocopying, recording or otherwise) without the prior written permission of the publisher.

To my mother, Joanne Porto Howe,
and my father, Peter Edward Howe (1953–2016):
Abbondanza.

CONTENTS

Introduction 1

Part 1: Sabbath Why
1. Egypt vs. God 11
2. What Israel Had to Learn 23
3. Jesus and the Sabbath 45
4. Our World, Work, and Freedom 50
5. Part 1 Recap 67

Part 2: Sabbath How
6. Worship 73
7. Feasting 93
8. Rest 121

9. Mercy 154
10. Ebenezer 178

Appendix 1: Pastors and Sabbaticals 188
Appendix 2: Sample Letters to Employers 199
Sources 206
Further Reading on Mercy and Charity 212

INTRODUCTION

IT WAS MORE THAN an hour's drive to the farm for Thanksgiving on Jackass Hill, and we got there mid-morning. Mom's Uncle Bob was a dairy farmer, and Aunt Irene was postmistress in the village of Erieville, New York. The dairy farm was old: the house and the old barn dated to the 1800s. (In good practical Upstate New York fashion, the unused part of the upstairs was plasticked off and had insulation spread on the floor to conserve some heat.)

The farm was the kind you find all over the Northeast, probably all over America. Bob kept maybe 100 head of Holsteins, and he loved being a farmer. Growing up in a Polish immigrant family near Syracuse, he had known from age three what he wanted to do and be, and he was doing and being it. Nearing retirement, Bob was increasingly turning the care of the herd over to his daughter Robyn and her husband, Dick.

Mom had spent summers on the farm as a child, playing with her cousin and getting into all the trouble rambunctious girls can get into. We in turn came to love visits with Bob and Irene, Robyn and Dick, and the cousins and aunts and uncles who gathered there for various holidays. Every visit included an insane hour or so playing in the hay barn, where kids climbed to and jumped from inconceivable heights, and always landed safely; a visit to the cows when they were being milked (stay away from their tails!); a walk through the shortcut cornfields, whether or not they were covered with snow; and, of course, dinner.

Bob would fall asleep in his easy chair, both before and after the meal, in the way of a farmer with a day off. There was football on TV, and it didn't really matter who was playing. Mom, her cousins, her aunts, and (when I was very young) Grandma were making a lot of noise in the kitchen: a visit with this side of the family was nothing if not raucous. And dinner was a feast. The only caution was that you had to look for lead pellets in the turkey, because Robyn shot it.

The biblical Sabbath looks a lot like a good Thanksgiving. It's a day of rest, leisure. There is still necessary work: the cows have to be milked no matter what the calendar says, and some amount of food preparation has to happen. But anything that can be set aside is set aside. It's not a day for catching up on work or homework, or taking on new projects. And no one really wants it to be. There is feasting—not just eating, but bringing people to the same table who otherwise wouldn't be eating together. Feasting isn't just food: it's fellowship. There is hospitality, welcoming those who would otherwise spend the day alone, and perhaps don't have much to feast on. And above all, although we have largely forgotten this at American Thanksgiving, there is worship. The day is called Thanks-giving and it is intended to celebrate God's goodness. And while worship is part of Thanksgiving Day's "identity," it is indispensable to keeping the Lord's Day.

Thanksgiving at Aunt Irene and Uncle Bob's was good. Shouldn't the Sabbath "taste" even better? But of course it doesn't always. More than a hundred years earlier, as described in Laura Ingalls Wilder's book *Farmer Boy*, another Upstate New York farm family was keeping Sunday holy as best they could. After an enormous midday dinner:

> Eliza Jane and Alice did the dishes, but Father and Mother and Royal and Almanzo did nothing at all. The whole afternoon they sat in the drowsy warm dining-room. Mother read the Bible and Eliza Jane read a book, and Father's head nodded till he woke

with a jerk, and then it began to nod again. Royal fingered the wooden chain that he could not whittle, and Alice looked for a long time out of the window. But Almanzo just sat. He had to. He was not allowed to do anything else, for Sunday was not a day for working or playing. It was a day for going to church and for sitting still.

Almanzo was glad when it was time to do the chores.

Now, there are some good things here. The family went to church in the morning. There is a good meal, and Dad nods off (something I appreciate more now, as a middle-aged dad, than I did as a youngster). But there is also an air of gloom about this description. Whether it is an accurate picture of 19th-century Sundays or not, this is exactly what many people think of when they think of Sabbath keeping: a pointless, boring thing to be endured before continuing the real business of life.

It should not be so. God's invitation to "call the Sabbath a delight" (Is. 58:13) is not a command to make-believe, like pretending quinoa is steak. It's a call to delight in something delightful, rich, life-giving—something given to us for our blessing and refreshment, not as a trial. I hope that in the course of this book you will start to feel that delight.

WHAT IS THE SABBATH?

At its simplest, the Sabbath is a day of rest that God appoints for us. Keeping it means resting and giving rest to others, as much as we can. We keep the Sabbath because God commands us to—but we can only understand the commandment by looking at the whole biblical story of salvation, Old Testament and New Testament.

For Sabbath rest to make sense we first have to see the restlessness of the world. What was true of ancient empires (Egypt, Babylon, and Rome) is true of us as well: we do not know how to be still, and we don't like to be still. The arrogance of the Tower of Babel, the slave-driving of Egypt, the hungry aggression of the Babylonians, and later the ruthless "peace" of the Romans, have much in common with the modern way of life: anxiety, ceaseless movement, a drive for achievement and greatness, oppression, lust for power, and an insatiable desire for more stuff.

If we see this restlessness clearly, then we can see the Sabbath as not just an ancient rule for Jews and Christians, but as the door to a different kind of world. The Sabbath leads us to look at life and everything we have as gifts, rather than scarce resources we have to fight and scrabble over. It calls us, not to a lazy life of porch sitting or a blur of constant toil and responsibility, but to a pattern of work and life-giving rest. It opens up to us God's alternative to slavery: independence and equality of opportunity for all, not as disconnected individuals, but as communities and especially as households. And best, the weekly Sabbath points us to *the* Sabbath: the rest that awaits all God's people, the rest that God enjoys himself, which we will enter if we persevere (Heb. 4:11).

In this book we'll walk through the biblical teaching on the Sabbath: first its Old Testament roots (particularly the exodus from Egypt) and later the questions that surrounded the Sabbath in Jesus's day, and his astonishing answers. We want to see the *why* of the Sabbath before we see the *how*. And when we get to the practical chapters, we'll look at the practice of Sabbath keeping under four words: worship, feasting, rest, and mercy.

Worship is the essential activity of Sabbath keeping for Christians. We are called to make this a priority, even in circumstances where we are forced to work much of the day. The practice of worship, something that involves our bodies as well as our hearts, when we gather in one place with other believers, is as basic to being a Christian as playing football is to being a football player. When we worship with other believers, we are obeying the Lord's command to "be still and know that I am God" (Ps. 46:10), which is the heart of the Sabbath.

Feasting makes the day a celebration and not a chore. We practice love for our neighbor as well as love for God. As well-fed modern people we don't appreciate feasting: we can't really feast because we don't fast. But the Bible links together worship and feasting, so that the Sabbath becomes truly a *holiday* ("holy day"), as Christmas or Thanksgiving are for most people. To practice the Sabbath we don't just stop working, we eat the fruit of our labor. This is pictured in the Bible as sitting under our "own vine and fig tree" (1 Kings 4:25), at peace and at rest, drinking wine and eating fruit.

Rest from our labors (Exod. 20:8–11; Deut. 5:12–15) is the most controversial (and neglected) part of keeping the Sabbath. We'll wrestle with important questions, such as whether Jesus kept the Sabbath, whether the early Christians rested on the first day of the week, and what our own practice should be. We will look at the use of technology, what is and isn't an emergency, and how to rest the body and the mind. We'll also examine the strenuous instructions of the Westminster documents (the most important theological guides for most Presbyterians) on Sabbath keeping and how to understand them in context and practice them today. We'll also look at workers facing special challenges, including doctors and nurses, less skilled laborers, and pastors.

Mercy is giving rest to others and is the point of most of the fourth commandment. While we are to personally enjoy Sabbath rest, we are called *even more* to let others within the reach of our choices rest: our families, our employees, and so on. We set aside our normal business: we don't make transactions we don't have to, and we don't rest at the expense of others' paid labor (waitresses, grocery stockers, and professional athletes). A merciful Sabbath means more than this, though: it also means helping or visiting the poor or practicing hospitality.

In a final short chapter we'll try to look at the big picture of Christian faith in the modern world. Western culture has moved, in a matter of decades, from mostly respecting Christianity to either ignoring it or viewing it with outright hostility. This change may feel like a one-way street, a done deal. Not so. God's commandment has not changed, and he understands the difficulty of our situations just as he understood that of the Hebrews in Egypt. Change in society begins as Christian families, individuals, and churches one by one decide it's okay to be weird, and maybe miss out on some things, in order to rest and give others rest. The revolution starts on Sunday—the Sabbath.

PART 1: SABBATH WHY

1
EGYPT VS. GOD

THE SABBATH BEGINS to make sense when we look at Egypt.

Genesis and Exodus are the first two books of the Bible and the first two books of the five law books of Moses (the *Torah*). Most biblical explorations of the Sabbath start with Genesis. That makes sense, because Genesis records the creation of the world and God's own Sabbath rest at the end of the creation days. It also makes sense because, if we are reading the Bible as new Christians or as children, we naturally start at the beginning.

The first readers (or hearers) of Exodus knew that story well: they were Israelites, probably living in the newly conquered Promised Land only a generation or two after God had brought them out of Egypt. But Genesis was (mostly) news to them, as it is to us. Genesis is the "prequel" to Exodus, giving background on the beginning of the world, the calling of Abraham, and the origin of Israel.

To understand the Sabbath, we have to spend some time in the story where the Sabbath made its first appearance to the nation of Israel. That story is the story of the exodus from Egypt and what followed: the giving of the Law and the conquest of Canaan. So instead of starting in Eden, we will start in Egypt.

THE JUGGERNAUT

Egypt was *the* great civilization of the very ancient world. For almost 3,000 years the nation had no serious challengers for its status as richest and mightiest. The military of Egypt was formidable, and though centuries later it would suffer defeat in battle with the Babylonians and other Middle Eastern empires, invasion was seldom a serious concern.

It was also a center of innovation in science, engineering, and agriculture. The construction of the great pyramids still puzzles historians: certainly there was nothing to rival them in the known world at the time. Egypt's wealth flowed, literally, from the Nile River. Each year the river flooded, bringing rich soil from the Ethiopian uplands and fertilizing the great farms of the Nile Delta. A complex series of dikes and dams captured the water, and grain

Egypt vs. God

was grown at large scale. During the first century AD the Roman Empire depended on Egypt so much for wheat that a series of crop failures there threatened starvation around the Mediterranean. Egyptians are credited with having invented beer, using a soupy, cloudy grain brew to supply countless workers with adequate calories. Beer after work began in ancient Egypt.

Everyone wanted to be like Egypt. In many ways other ancient empires—the Hittites, Assyrians, Babylonians, Persians—were imitators. They came and went in Mesopotamia and Persia, but Egypt seemed eternal. This longevity was partly a result of geology: its great cities and monuments were built of sandstone and limestone from the Nile Valley. The cities and palaces of Mesopotamia were often built entirely of mud bricks, and hundred-year floods washed them away entirely from time to time.

And Egypt was, and is, *cool*. Cool like modern architecture: spare, clean lines, hard edges, a bit alien and inhuman. Camille Paglia writes, "Egypt invented the magic of *image*. . . . Egypt invented glamour, beauty as power and power as beauty. Egyptian aristocrats were the first Beautiful People." Every other civilization has its look, but few have the perfect geometry and style of the Egyptians, and none at such an enormous scale. They make the thickly bearded Assyrian kings, boasting of conquests and lion hunts on their memorial carvings, seem like they're trying too hard.

FARMS AND CULTURE

Every civilization is built on farming. This is true even though cities are usually the centers of art and literature. Culture requires cultivation of the soil. With a steady supply of food (normally grain), people could stay in one place, rather than moving with their grazing herds or the game they hunt. In fact, they had to stay in one place, because they had fields to tend. Over time, some farmers were more successful than others, allowing them to spend time and resources on art, tools, buildings, or writing. Most technologies (tools) were developed to make either farming or war more successful.

The twelve sons of Israel moved into Egypt without a background as farmers. Up until that point they had been successful nomadic herdsmen (Gen. 32:13–21). But during a famine, Egyptian farming looked like the key to success. After all, inspired by Pharaoh's dreams of cattle and ears of wheat, his chief manager, Joseph, had managed to store enough grain to get the nation *and its neighbors* through a seven-year famine. He took advantage of the crisis to buy much of Egypt's farmland for Pharaoh, selling back to starving farmers what had been taxed from them in previous years (Gen. 47:13–26). When they left 400 years later, the descendants of Israel had multiplied, and they were farmers.

Not only did Pharaoh own the land, he effectively enslaved much of the population (Gen. 47:19). Egypt had a powerful central government and a command economy, much like a communist nation, but without any pretense of belonging to "the people." Government and business were identical. The wealth and centralized power of Egypt made a powerful statement: men had risen to the level of gods. The world and everything good in it was the achievement of mankind, under the command of a divine ruler and his or her bureaucratic elite. While Egypt usually (not always) worshiped many gods, one god was always front and center: the Pharaoh.

Moses, writing Genesis and Exodus, is clear: when Israel entered Egypt, the time of epic heroes was over. No more Nephilim (Gen. 6:4), no more Nimrod (Gen. 10:8), no more Gilgamesh. In large and sophisticated empires, the smart succeed: planners and engineers, like those responsible for the grand building projects; magicians and wise men, the economists and statisticians of Egypt and Babylon; managers and gifted administrators, like Joseph. "Then Pharaoh said to Joseph, 'Since God has shown you all this, there is none so discerning and wise as you are. You shall be over my house, and all my people shall order themselves as you command. Only as regards the throne will I be greater than you'" (Gen. 41:39–40).

In the hundreds of years after Joseph died, the people of Israel grew in number and were eventually enslaved and put to work on royal building projects. To us, Egypt is best known for monuments like the pyramids, the Valley of the Kings, and so on. Many of these buildings were tombs, a sign of the pharaohs' anxiety for immortality.

But none of these are mentioned in the Bible. Exodus specifically tells us that the Hebrews built the "store cities, Pithom and Raamses" (Exod. 1:11). Pharaoh was not stupid, but a long-term thinker who was intelligent and ruthless. Just like his predecessor, who had given much authority to Joseph the wise administrator, he wanted to build for the future strength and stability of Egypt, as well as his own glory. So he prepared for future famines. But in his arrogance he refused to humble himself when a *real* threat to Egypt came along: Moses, bearing God's demand that Pharaoh "Let my people go" (Exod. 5:1). Like the rich fool in Jesus's parable, he stored up treasure for himself (Luke 12:21). And in the end, it was the anxiety of Egypt that Israel learned, not its extravagance.

Egypt was oppressive, and Pharaoh was a tyrant. The land belonged to Pharaoh: everyone else was just a tenant. You do not own your own land and farm (even with a mortgage); you cannot inherit it; you rent from Pharaoh. It's no surprise, then, that Pharaoh believed he could own the Hebrews and their children as well. Fearing the growing number of Hebrew workers, Pharaoh enslaved them (Exod. 1:8–11). Perhaps in response, the Hebrews multiplied even more. So Pharaoh attempted population control.

At first he tried to keep it quiet, instructing the chief midwives to strangle the male infants they helped birth. But they would not obey, so Pharaoh resorted to overt genocide: commanding that male Israelite children be thrown into the sacred and life-giving Nile, to drown or be eaten by crocodiles.

UNLEARNING EGYPT

Strange to say, Israel profited greatly from their time in Egypt. They grew in number: "Your fathers went down to Egypt seventy persons, and now the Lord your God has made you as numerous as the stars of heaven" (Deut. 10:22). Exodus records that "the people of Israel journeyed from Rameses to Succoth, about six hundred thousand men on foot, besides women and children" (Exod. 12:37). They learned agriculture. The skills of farming would be absolutely essential for settled life in the land of Canaan, which God had promised to their ancestors Abraham, Isaac, and Jacob (all nomadic herders). They even left with their arms full of gold and jewels from Egyptians desperate to see them leave the morning after the Passover.

But Israel had things to *unlearn* from their time in Egypt as well. Farming and the civilization it made provided them with powerful tools, not only for survival, but for ruling Canaan, trading, gathering wealth, and taking advantage of each other. In Egypt they had seen wealth, splendor, and power. They had also seen onions: "We remember the fish we ate in Egypt that cost nothing," they complain to Moses later, "the cucumbers, the melons, the leeks, the onions, and the garlic" (Num. 11:5). It didn't take long for the Hebrews to miss the material comforts of their captivity, and forget the whips and infanticide.

While in Egypt, the Israelites forgot (or all but forgot) their spiritual ancestry. God—Yahweh, "He Who Is"—had made a covenant bond with the patriarchs, and on the basis of his own promised grace came to rescue their descendants. But over the years they had begun to worship the local idols. Joshua, at the end of his long life and decades after the exodus, warned: "Put away the gods that your fathers served beyond the River and in Egypt, and serve the Lord" (Josh. 24:14). There is every reason to believe that most Israelites, at least until the Babylonian exile eight centuries later, continued to worship an array of household idols. And that's not to mention the worship of Canaanite gods and other gods that they came across in the Promised Land.

The period of the Judges, following the conquest of Canaan, was a mess. "In those days there was no king in Israel. Everyone did what was right in his own eyes" (Judg. 17:6). So it was no surprise that the nation eventually petitioned Samuel, probably the most effective of the judges, to ask the Lord for a king. Samuel warned them:

"These will be the ways of the king who will reign over you: he will take your sons and appoint them to his chariots and to be his horsemen and to run before his chariots. And he will appoint for himself commanders of thousands and commanders of fifties, and some to plow his ground and to reap his harvest, and to make his implements of war and the equipment of his chariots. He will take your daughters to be perfumers and cooks and bakers. He will take the best of your fields and vineyards and olive orchards and give them to his servants. He will take the tenth of your grain and of your vineyards and give it to his officers and to his servants. He will take your male servants and female servants and the best of your young men and your donkeys, and put them to his work. He will take the tenth of your flocks, and you shall be his slaves. And in that day you will cry out because of your king, whom you have chosen for yourselves, but the LORD will not answer you in that day." (1 Sam. 8:11–18)

God warned that the king they wanted so badly would become a homegrown pharaoh, confiscating crops and people, not only to rule them and lead them in battle (which they wanted), but also to enrich himself and his friends. This is exactly what happened. From Solomon onward, the kings of united Israel and later of Judah worked hard to centralize in Jerusalem the religious life of the nation (good) and all of the politics, administration, and business of the kingdom (not so good). Hezekiah, shortly before the exile, sent Sennacherib of Assyria a tribute payment of 300 talents of silver and 30 talents of gold—an enormous sum of money (2 Kings 18:14). Yet only a few years later, his royal bank had recovered so completely that he was showing off his rich treasuries to envoys from Babylon (a foolish move, as it turned out).

Money and power do not always corrupt, but they almost always do. The Law and Proverbs of Israel warn against oppression of the poor throughout the land. But as time passed, it was the royal houses of Samaria and Jerusalem that came in for the most criticism, and their greatest critics were the prophets. Elijah, Elisha, Jeremiah, and a host of others blasted all nations, but especially Israel, led by royalty and ruling elites, for their love of luxury, idol worship, oppression of the poor, and sexual immorality. These sins were tied together (and still are). They were the ways of Egypt that God's people should have shaken off long before.

EMPIRE OF ANXIETY

We want to control our own lives, ensure against disaster, and control or at least predict the future. Planning ahead is good, but only when it is done with humility and prayer for God's help. Remember that, like a giant corporation sitting on billions in cash, Egypt leveraged its past successes (confiscating land and enslaving workers) to hedge against the future, building not just storehouses but store *cities*.

This helps us understand a little incident in the desert of Sinai following the exodus. To provide for their daily needs, God had sent the daily miracle of manna into the camp of Israel. Every day it appeared on the ground with the dew. Each person had as much as he or she needed for the day, and they were not allowed to store the leftovers. They needed to trust God to provide again in the morning. (The exception was the sixth day of the week, when the Lord sent twice as much manna and told them to store half for the Sabbath.) Moses warned them, "'Let no one leave any of it over till the morning.' But they did not listen to Moses. Some left part of it till the morning, and it bred worms and stank. And Moses was angry with them" (Exod. 16:19–20).

Author and scholar Walter Brueggemann points out that, for all its wealth and might, Egypt was an empire of anxiety. Pharaoh had no god higher than himself, in whom he could trust and on whom he could call. Israel learned his brand of anxious care: no one will provide for my needs if I don't do it myself. A healthy message of self-reliance becomes gnawing worry if there is no God above.

Israel needed to unlearn the restlessness of Egypt. God made us for times of work and times of rest. People who are restless not only can't rest, they can't properly work, either. Sloth and restlessness are sides of the same coin. In each case, there is a refusal of the gift God has put before us. The slothful person won't embrace the gift of work. The restless person won't accept the gift of rest. These are not just individual issues: entire peoples can be gripped by one or the other (or both). The characteristic sickness of a great empire is its anxiety, its restlessness. Silicon Valley investor Naval Ravikant tweeted: "Doctors won't make you healthy. Nutritionists won't make you slim. Teachers won't make you smart. Gurus won't make you calm. Mentors won't make you rich. Trainers won't make you fit. Ultimately, you have to take responsibility. *Save yourself*" (italics added). There is truth in this message: all but the last two words.

Arguably, those two words are at the root of all sin. "You are less than you could be," whispered the serpent to Eve: "Save yourself." Idolatry is another form of saving yourself: "Serve this image of what you need so very much, and it will help you." "It's kill or be killed in this economy; the law of the jungle. Save yourself." When we cannot or will not entrust ourselves to the living God, the ways of Egypt are alive in us, too, and we need to unlearn them.

2
WHAT ISRAEL HAD TO LEARN

THE ONLY WAY TO LEAVE an old way of life behind is to learn a new one. It wasn't enough to stop living like Egyptians: God's people had to walk a new path.

So what and how *did* Israel learn about the restlessness of the world and about God's rest? First, they learned *from the exodus itself.* God hated the ways of Egypt. He made war on Egypt's wealth at its source, the Nile, by turning its water to blood in the first of ten plagues. He made war on Pharaoh's claim of ultimate rule over his nation by ravaging the land and freeing the Hebrews. He revealed that Pharaoh did not control life and death, killing the infanticidal king's own firstborn as well as the firstborn of all Egypt. The Lord made war on Egypt's gods, especially Pharaoh, showing that they were helpless before his power.

Israel had to relearn what fathers Abraham, Isaac, and Jacob knew: that there is only one true God. In defeating Pharaoh and the gods of Egypt, God claimed Israel for his own—"I will walk among you and will be your God, and you shall be my people" (Lev. 26:12). They learned in both the exodus and the conquest of Canaan that salvation is a gift. The exodus was not an uprising. Israel did nothing to save themselves: given how much they grumbled, we might say they did less than nothing. Entering the Promised Land they found themselves in a land that had already been cleared and cultivated, yielding food they had done nothing to raise.

In Canaan, Israel learned that the world does not work as it appeared to in Egypt. The Promised Land was not irrigated by a great river that topped its banks once a year, but by rain:

> For the land that you are entering to take possession of it is not like the land of Egypt, from which you have come, where you sowed your seed and irrigated it, like a garden of vegetables. But the land that you are going over to possess is a land of hills and valleys, which drinks water by the rain from heaven, a land that the LORD your God cares for. The eyes of the LORD your God are always upon

it, from the beginning of the year to the end of the
year. (Deut. 11:10–12)

Though they farmed in Egypt as slaves, the farming was relatively *easy:* no crop rotation, no watching the sky for rain, flat land. Now they would have to work differently, plan differently, and pray for God's blessing.

In Egypt the government was centralized; in Canaan it would be local. While judges "arose" to offer wisdom and sometimes lead in battle (Judg. 10:1, 3), there was no capital city until Saul was king in Gibeah (1 Sam. 15:34). There were chiefs of tribes and clans, "fathers' houses," and families. Leaders at every level were responsible to observe and enforce the law of God. Life in Canaan was humble, difficult, and sometimes dangerous—but it was free. There was no more command economy. Early on, the Israelites paid no regular taxes, farmed their own lands, and were protected from much interference. Like the ancient Greeks or colonial Americans, they banded together for defense. Unlike the Greeks or Americans, they fought no wars of expansion after the initial holy war of conquest. They knew the boundaries of the land God had given them.

THE LAW OF MOSES

Next, *Israel learned from God's law*. The first five books of the Bible are together called the Law. That means that not only the commandments, but also every story in those books, were given to teach Israel, and us, about God and how to live in the world.

The Law teaches that everyone—the migrant worker, the hired hand, the indentured servant, the livestock, the kids—has a right to Sabbath rest. Even if they work like a slave all week, even if they *are* a slave, they are to enjoy this weekly gift. And the Sabbath teaches about the fundamental reality of the world. It is not a place of endless work where we are defined by what we do or what we are paid. It is a world of grace: our situation and identity are decided by God, and the end of all our labors will be joy and gladness.

"Six days you shall labor, and do all your work, but the seventh day is a Sabbath to the Lord your God. On it you shall not do any work, you, or your son, or your daughter, your male servant, or your female servant, or your livestock, or the sojourner who is within your gate" (Exod. 20:9–10). The Ten Commandments are given twice in the books of Moses: once just after leaving Egypt and once just before entering the Promised Land. The two records are nearly identical, but they differ when it comes to explaining the Sabbath. While in Exodus, the commandment is tied to creation, in Deuteronomy it is rooted in the memory of slavery:

> For in six days the Lord made heaven and earth,
> the sea, and all that is in them, and rested on the

seventh day. Therefore the Lord blessed the Sabbath day and made it holy. (Exod. 20:11)

You shall remember that you were a slave in the land of Egypt, and the Lord your God brought you out from there with a mighty hand and an outstretched arm. Therefore the Lord your God commanded you to keep the Sabbath day. (Deut. 5:15)

The Sabbath means more than setting aside daily labors, but it does not mean less. For the Israelite family or clan, this was the straightforward practice of the Sabbath: no unnecessary labor on the seventh day of the week for anyone in their realm of influence.

Always holding onto the memory of slavery in Egypt, *the Law taught just treatment of outsiders and the poor.* Their past was to shape how Israel treated foreign "sojourners" (probably resident workers with no plans to become Israelites): "You shall not wrong a sojourner or oppress him, for you were sojourners in the land of Egypt" (Exod. 22:21). And then in Leviticus 19:13: "You shall treat the stranger who sojourns with you as the native among you, and you shall love him as yourself, for you were strangers in the land of Egypt: I am the Lord your God" (Lev. 19:34). For the same reason, there was to be no ripping off fellow Israelites: "You shall not oppress your neighbor or rob him. The wages of a hired worker shall not remain with you all night until the morning."

In our culture most people are hired workers, working for wages in someone else's business. But for ancient Israel a hired worker was a poor person, someone down on his luck, possibly landless, or someone whose farm had failed to produce enough food to support his family's needs. (By Jesus's day 1,400 years later, most small farmers were *also* hired workers, struggling to pay heavy religious fees as well as ruinous Roman taxes.)

The Law taught that everyone should get enough. Every tribe (except Levi) had its own allotment of land, divided among clans and families. Each of these allotments was passed down through families. Allotments that had been sold had to be returned to the original family, free of charge (Lev. 25:10). If someone was without land (short- or long-term), he or she had a right to "glean," that is, to harvest the corners of the grain fields and unpicked fruit from vines and trees. "And when you reap the harvest of your land, you shall not reap your field right up to its edge, nor shall you gather the gleanings after your harvest. You shall leave them for the poor and for the sojourner: I am the LORD your God" (Lev. 23:22).

All of this meant that there were serious limits on anyone's opportunities either to get very rich *or* stay very poor. We may feel uncomfortable with the idea that God loves equality and limits opportunity (although Jesus does much the same thing by limiting marriage to one man and one woman). But consider the wisdom here: instead of pursuing equality the modern way, taxing like Pharaoh and then redistributing money, *God's law distributes the opportunity to work and raise food.*

This kind of equality is also connected with the Sabbath. Well-off people can usually rest when they like. But in God's economy, all rest together at his command. "Six days you shall do your work, but on the seventh day you shall rest; that your ox and your donkey may have rest, and the son of your servant woman, and the alien, may be refreshed" (Exod. 23:12). Rest was to happen on *God's* schedule—not Pharaoh's, not the company's, not yours. Why? To put all people on an equal footing, to protect the most vulnerable, and to make it clear that God is the true source of all rest and blessing.

The message of Egypt was that all were dependent on Pharaoh for a living and a future. He even decided if his people lived or died: Pharaoh giveth, and Pharaoh taketh away; blessed be the name of Pharaoh. In answer, the law of God taught Israel that we are entirely in God's hands. We do not need to be geniuses, able to see into the future and make clever decisions, and we do not need to grovel before Pharaoh or any earthly power. If we fear God, we need fear nothing and no one else. This does not make us rebels. Israel, and we, are still called to honor father and mother, the elderly, government, and authorities of various kinds. Centuries later the apostle Peter wrote, "Honor everyone.

Love the brotherhood. Fear God. Honor the emperor" (1 Peter 2:17). But the blasphemous claims of Pharaoh and many other rulers, that they are gods or ought to be honored like gods, cannot stand. The future is in God's hands. We work when he commands us, pray for our daily bread, and rest in his care.

Finally, *the Law taught these former slaves that they had dignity*. "I am the LORD your God, who brought you out of the land of Egypt, that you should not be their slaves. And I have broken the bars of your yoke and made you walk erect" (Lev. 26:13). The Sabbath confirmed this message. Workplaces can be tyrannical and abusive, or they can be happy and healthy. But all workplaces are, like armies, hierarchies. Some people are in charge, and other people report to them. On a holiday, the world changes. The rich and the poor alike stand next to each other at the tree lighting ceremony downtown. Everyone is barbecuing and playing cornhole on Memorial Day, whether they're at the yacht club or the public park. In rest and play, the dignity and equality of mankind reappear. We all walk tall.

CREATION

At last, we're in a good place to talk about the prequel: what Israel learned from the story of creation and particularly, the institution of the Sabbath. Having finished his work of creation in six days, God rested:

Thus the heavens and the earth were finished, and all the host of them. And on the seventh day God finished his work that he had done, and he rested on the seventh day from all his work that he had done. So God blessed the seventh day and made it holy, because on it God rested from all his work that he had done in creation. (Gen. 2:1–3)

When Jesus wanted to correct the Pharisees' views on marriage and divorce, he took them back to creation (Matt. 19:8). Moses did the same in the books of Exodus and Genesis, correcting the Israelites' damaged Egyptian understanding of work and rest. The story of the creation has many purposes, but one of them is to give us a pattern for work and life: six days of labor and one of restful enjoyment and reflection. Each day the Lord begins like a farmer or a craftsman, looking at the field or the raw material in front of him, putting his hands to it, and working it into something better. Almost every day ends with, "and God saw that it was good." He ceases his work and begins again the next day. When the week's work is done, "God saw everything that he made, and behold, it was very good" (Gen. 1:31).

Absolutely none of this was necessary. God did not *need* to create the world at all. He did not *need* to spread the work of creation over six days, and he certainly did not *need* to rest. But like a wise father teaching his children some simple skill, he modeled faithful labor and rest for the children he made in his image. We would not have learned the week without this. Day and night are natural; months are ruled by the moon; seasons and years are marked out by the movement of the sun. But the week is not something we learn from nature. It has to be taught. Just like a farmer works with and respects nature, but imposes his plans and desires on the land, the week of work and rest is imposed on the world by the action of God. We follow his lead.

What does it mean for God to rest? As we'll see later, it's not simply "absence of activity" (although it does mean setting aside many of our regular tasks). My late father was a gardener and the son of a gardener (after returning from World War II, my grandfather founded both a rifle club and a men's garden club in Syracuse, New York). Dad did not do anything to his garden on Sunday. But he did like to walk around his flowers, beans, and potatoes after Sunday dinner, enjoying what God had given him strength and skill to do during the week. This is exactly the picture in Genesis 1–2. God has done very good work. On the Sabbath he enjoys it. Rest is setting down our work to admire and enjoy it, in imitation of God. Rest crowns work.

But biblical rest is better than that. As God's children we enjoy *his* work when we rest. We all know what it is like to have a project fail. Those who garden or farm know what it is like to have plants or livestock die. Unless the Lord sends the rain and sun, and keeps the bugs and mildew at bay, our land will not "yield its increase," (Ps. 85:12). The chainsaw carburetor will refuse to get clean. The sump pump will quit. We'll cut off some fingers while using a tool. It is not our hard work or good luck that stands between us and injury, disaster, starvation: it's the lavish kindness of God, whose mercies are "new every morning" (Lam. 3:23). Biblical rest is a celebration of God's sending the sun and the rain, keeping grubs from the roots, filling the well with clean water, making our clothes last another season, strengthening the framing of the old house so that it doesn't fall down.

Wise people, Christian and not, know how important it is to step back from work and reflect. This is true whether we work at a desk, in a factory, in the home, or in a field. Work without letup is worse than slavery: it's the front porch of hell. "But the wicked are like the tossing sea; for it cannot be quiet, and its waters toss up mire and dirt. There is no peace . . . for the wicked" (Isa. 57:20–21).

But rest, enjoying the blessing of God on our work, is a taste of heaven. This becomes even clearer when we look at what comes after the Sabbath verses early in Genesis 2. We read about the formation of Adam and Eve and their placement in the garden God planted in Eden.

> Out of the ground the Lord God made to spring up every tree that is pleasant to the sight and good for

food. The tree of life was in the midst of the garden, and the tree of the knowledge of good and evil. A river flowed out of Eden to water the garden, and there it divided and became four rivers. . . . The Lord God took the man and put him in the garden of Eden to work it and keep it. (Gen. 2:9–10, 15)

A little later, God made the woman, a "helper fit for him" (Gen. 2:20).

Adam and Eve were given a "cultural mandate" with several sides. They were to "be fruitful and multiply and fill the earth," that is, have children. They were to "subdue" the earth and "have dominion" over other living creatures (Gen. 1:28). Yet they were also put in a garden and told to "work it and keep it." At first glance these might appear to be the same jobs, but they are not. Man was given outward-facing tasks of farming and filling the world. But he was also told to care for and guard the garden. When we think of a garden, we should not think of a glorified field or a mere patch of vegetables. In the ancient East, gardens were literally the heart of civilization. They were always surrounded by walls, and were filled with beauty and good smells: flowers and aromatic spice trees as well as fruit trees, vines, and vegetables. Normally they had a stream or a fountain watering them. The garden was the best part of any ancient house. The Babylonian kings and other royals built palaces that were also gardens, and filled them with exotic plants, pavilions for feasting, and often a zoo or aviary.

To be put in a garden God had planted meant that the first man and woman were not starting from scratch. When they opened their eyes they found themselves *already in civilization*, already provided with good things to eat, flowing water, and living, growing beauty. They lived in a world of abundance, not scarcity. Moses's readers and hearers would have heard an echo of God's provision for them: like Israel in Canaan, Adam and Eve found themselves in a land that had already been cleared and cultivated, yielding food they had done nothing to raise. They were still to pursue civilization—having kids, cultivating, building, inventing—but they were to do this in a land that God had already blessed and caused to bear fruit.

What does this have to do with us and the Sabbath? Everything. Some people approach life as a war to be fought, and the world as an enemy, or as a "blank slate" on which to create something new. They worry that if they don't keep pushing, driving, and fighting, everything they have will slip away. Psalm 127 speaks to this attitude: "It is in vain that you rise up early and go late to rest, eating the bread of anxious toil; for he gives his beloved sleep" (Ps. 127:2). We *are* called to build and cultivate, and sometimes to push, drive, or fight. But our starting point is not "nothing." We live in God's rich world. No one starts from scratch. No one pulls himself up by his bootstraps. That's hard on the human ego. We want to think that we earned what we have.

In God's kindness, he may have let us contribute to the success we enjoy through the work he gives us to do. But it could have been otherwise. We could have been "birds of the air: they neither sow nor reap nor gather into barns, and yet your heavenly Father feeds them" (Matt. 6:26). Anxiety makes no sense in God's world. If he has given us all that we have and know as a gift, then it does not depend on our labors. And if our lives and the world don't depend on our labors, then we can rest when it's time to rest.

There's another reason why it's important to see that Adam and Eve found themselves in a garden planted by God. Myths abound, ancient and modern, about how man made himself. The Greeks spoke of Prometheus stealing fire from the gods. Modern scientists imagine that primitive man "domesticated himself" through cooking food with fire (*Catching Fire* by Richard Wrangham), long-distance running (*Born to Run* by Christopher McDougall), growing grain (*Sapiens* by Yuval Noah Harari), or even brewing beer (*A Brief History of Vice* by Robert Evans). By our own drive and ingenuity, the story goes, we created ourselves. Some go on to say that it is up to us to continue our evolution, becoming a more advanced, perhaps an immortal version of humanity (an idea called "transhumanism").

It is tempting to think this way. After all, there are a lot of us in the world today: probably a hundred times as many as in Moses's day. And there is no doubt that our lives and our planet have changed radically through the technologies of the last few hundred years. Internet pioneer and *Whole Earth Catalog* author Stewart Brand said in the 1960s, "We are as gods and might as well get good at it."

But we are not gods. We are not able to bear that weight. God warns the powerful of the earth: "I said, 'You are gods, sons of the Most High, all of you; nevertheless, like men you shall die, and fall like any prince'" (Ps. 82:6–7). Our relative power, as modern people, makes us more responsible for our actions, not less. The people of Babel were confused in their languages and scattered for the same arrogance. The power we have, or think we have, will not save us from the judgment of the true and living God. The Sabbath teaches us a different way: humility and thankfulness toward the one who made us and the world we live in.

Finally, the creation account teaches that *all* people are called to Sabbath rest. As the account of the beginning of human life, what is true for humanity at creation is true for all humanity since. We are called to rest as God did, one day in seven. This is not a rule for Israel alone, any more than marriage was. We are called to trust that God will provide for seven days' need using only six days' labor. We are called to make a meaningful sacrifice to the Creator: just as Noah later offered up one of every seven clean animals, we offer one of every seven days. The world of Genesis 1–2, not the world of Egypt, is our home. We live in a world of God-given plenty, not scarcity. We have a task of cultivation, not self-invention, and our work must be punctuated by rest, in expectation that God will care for us.

THE KINGS AND THE PROPHETS

What Israel experienced in Egypt was never quite forgotten, but the later books of the Old Testament show that the ways of Egypt were a temptation for many. As Samuel had warned, the kings of Israel and Judah centralized power and money in their capital cities (Samaria and Jerusalem). King Ahab of Israel is an example of the wickedness the prophets spoke against. Ahab, who had been expanding his own estate by buying up local properties, cast his eye on the vineyard of his neighbor Naboth. He offers to buy it but Naboth declines: "The Lord forbid that I should give you the inheritance of my fathers" (1 Kings 21:3). The fact that Naboth will not sell him his ancestral land sends Ahab into a sulk. His wife Jezebel arranges for false witnesses to denounce Naboth as a traitor and blasphemer. In short order, Naboth is stoned to death and Ahab takes possession of his vineyard.

Walter Brueggemann points out that the restless covetousness of Pharaoh is alive and well in Ahab. He is not content to be king or to have the property he has, but wants what belongs to his neighbor as well. Isaiah speaks against this covetousness: "Woe to those who join house to house, who add field to field, until there is no more room, and you are made to dwell alone in the midst of the land" (Isa. 5:8). Micah says much the same: "Woe to those who devise wickedness and work evil on their beds! When the morning dawns, they perform it, because it is in the power of their hand. They covet fields and seize them, and houses, and take them away; they oppress a man and his house, a man and his inheritance" (Mic. 2:1–2). Many of those who piled up land and wealth also led the nation in idol worship. This included Ahab, who promoted the worship of the fertility god Baal and persecuted prophets of the Lord almost out of existence. This is not a coincidence.

The prophets witnessed that God's people must not be like Egypt. Rulers must serve the people, not their own wealth and power. They must uphold justice and the right to work, and in Israel and Judah, that meant protecting the ancient land rights. Man and animal must be given rest. Isaiah takes aim at those who plot and discuss their pursuit of wealth when they are supposedly fasting and keeping the Sabbath, and expect that their outward religion will buy them God's favor:

> "Why have we fasted, and you see it not?
> > Why have we humbled ourselves, and you take
> > > no knowledge of it?"

> Behold, in the day of your fast you seek your own
>   pleasure,
>   and oppress all your workers.
> Behold, you fast only to quarrel and to fight
>   and to hit with a wicked fist.
> Fasting like yours this day
>   will not make your voice to be heard on high.
> Is such the fast that I choose,
>   a day for a person to humble himself?
> Is it to bow down his head like a reed,
>   and to spread sackcloth and ashes under him?
> Will you call this a fast,
>   and a day acceptable to the Lord? (Isa. 58:3–5)

Later in the passage it becomes clear that not only their fasts but also their Sabbath keeping is empty, outward religion. The oppressors are fooling themselves into thinking that God will see and be pleased with their worship but be blind to their sins.

> If you turn back your foot from the Sabbath,
>   from doing your pleasure on my holy day,
> and call the Sabbath a delight
>   and the holy day of the Lord honorable;
> if you honor it, not going your own ways,
>   or seeking your own pleasure, or talking idly;

then you shall take delight in the LORD,
>   and I will make you ride on the heights of the
>   earth;
> I will feed you with the heritage of Jacob your father,
>   for the mouth of the LORD has spoken.
>
> (Isa. 58:13–14)

And so we are confronted with a deeper teaching about the Sabbath: it is not only a matter of the body and of outward practices, but a matter of the heart. It must never be kept hypocritically and as a cover for evil.

The era of the kings of Israel and Judah did not end well. First Israel in the 700s BC, then Judah in the 500s BC, were conquered by foreign empires (Assyria and Babylon) and their people deported. For Israel there would be no coming back. For Judah, many would return after a half century or so, but it would be long before Jerusalem reached its former splendor, and a descendant of David would never again sit on the throne of earthly Jerusalem.

In Exodus 23:10–11, Moses mandated that even the land was to have Sabbath rest every seventh year. The book of 2 Chronicles ends its account of the Babylonian conquest of Jerusalem this way:

> [The king of Babylon] took into exile in Babylon those who had escaped from the sword, and they

became servants to him and to his sons until the establishment of the kingdom of Persia, to fulfill the word of the LORD by the mouth of Jeremiah, *until the land had enjoyed its Sabbaths. All the days that it lay desolate it kept Sabbath, to fulfill seventy years.* (2 Chron. 36:20–21, emphasis added)

In the centuries since the exodus and Israel's settlement in Canaan, the commandment to give the land rest had never been kept. Restless work. Covetous business. Idolatrous worship. Debts had to be paid.

So, in the era of the kings and the prophets, yet another lesson had to be learned: the Sabbath is a warning. If we do not rest and give others rest when God calls us to, we will be *forced* to rest. That might be a war, an international deportation, a month in the hospital, an early death, or a pandemic lockdown. People who strive without resting and giving thanks will learn the hard way to stop striving.

There's one more lesson to learn from the time of the exile. Toward the end of his harrowing career, the prophet Jeremiah, still living in Judah, wrote a letter to the Jewish exiles in Babylon. Some of the prophets among the exiles were telling them, in effect, not to unpack: God wouldn't make them stay there long; surely he would bring them home. Not so, said the Lord through Jeremiah:

What Israel Had to Learn

> Thus says the LORD of hosts, the God of Israel, to all the exiles whom I have sent into exile from Jerusalem to Babylon: Build houses and live in them; plant gardens and eat their produce. Take wives and have sons and daughters; take wives for your sons, and give your daughters in marriage, that they may bear sons and daughters; multiply there, and do not decrease. But seek the welfare of the city where I have sent you into exile, and pray to the Lord on its behalf, for in its welfare you will find your welfare. (Jer. 29:4–7)

This is a famous passage and I won't go deep into it. But look at a few details. First, the God of Israel claims that his people are in exile *because he sent them there.* No credit is given to the Babylonians for their military prowess, and there is no hint that God was helpless to stop the deportation. They are where God has put them and where he wants them.

Second, there are echoes of Genesis 2 throughout these verses. Work your gardens. Be fruitful and multiply. In other words: carry out the creation mandates, even in a hostile foreign land. Actually, *especially* in a hostile foreign land. The nerve of Jeremiah! And of anyone who would follow his instructions! They were going to treat Babylon like it was the garden of Eden. Dragged from their home into captivity, they were going to act like they owned the place. And in the years to come, that's exactly what they did. Faithfulness in Persia or Greece or Italy looked somewhat different than it did in the Holy Land, of course: the farming life that Moses prepared his people for was mostly gone, along with some of the festivals, sacrifices, and seasons. These were tied to the land of Canaan and to the temple. But one festival could be practiced anywhere. It was possible to keep the Sabbath in every land, and faithful Jews did, wherever they went.

3
JESUS AND THE SABBATH

THE ROOTS OF THE SABBATH are in creation and the exodus. But the Sabbath extends its branches far beyond those events. When some of the Babylonian exiles returned to Jerusalem, Nehemiah—governor of the Persian province that contained the city—oversaw a recovery of the law of Moses, including enforcement of the Sabbath. In the lands where Jews settled, they kept the Sabbath seriously, along with seriously rejecting idolatry (perhaps for the first time since leaving Egypt). The Sabbath became the anchor of a new, synagogue-based life and religion, not only in foreign lands but also in Judah (soon called Judea) and other parts of ancient Canaan.

By the time of Jesus, four centuries after Nehemiah, a new set of problems was coming to a head. The problem the

Old Testament writers and leaders faced was, for the most part, a refusal to keep the Sabbath. Nehemiah threatened violence against merchants who thought they could wait him out and continue their Sabbath trading in Jerusalem: "Why do you lodge outside the wall? If you do so again, I will lay hands on you" (Neh. 13:21). The new problem, touched on by Isaiah but relatively rare in the Old Testament, was a legalistic and hypocritical keeping of the Sabbath.

Centuries of complex arguments about what constituted keeping and breaking the Sabbath led to a somewhat absurd list of rules, exceptions, and loopholes, some of which are preserved in Orthodox and ultra-Orthodox Jewish practices today. These discussions mostly lost the point of the Sabbath, which is to enjoy God's rest and let others enjoy it as well. What Jesus said of the Pharisees' tithing practice could well be said of their Sabbath keeping: "Woe to you, scribes and Pharisees, hypocrites! For you tithe mint and dill and cumin, and have neglected the weightier matters of the Law: justice and mercy and faithfulness. These you ought to have done, without neglecting the others" (Matt. 23:23).

The practice of the Sabbath, just like the practice of tithing, should lead us straight to "justice and mercy and faithfulness." We should never think of Sabbath keeping as simply an area of personal holiness and purity. Jesus didn't.

The message of Jesus in his preaching was that the kingdom of God was at hand. The coming of the "Son of Man" (as he often called himself) meant a turning point in the history of the world. God's long-promised grace and salvation had arrived for Israel—but not only for Israel. The works Jesus did were not random "miracles." He didn't turn the sky green or turn pumpkins into carriages. They were *signs*, demonstrating not just the truth of his message but the nature of the kingdom. In the kingdom, there is no more blindness (spiritual or physical), so Jesus gave sight to the blind. In the kingdom, the hungry will be filled, so Jesus fed thousands with an armful of bread and fish.

So both the fact that Jesus kept the Sabbath and *how* he kept the Sabbath are significant. At one point, passing by a field, Jesus and his disciples picked some ripe heads of grain, rubbed them to get the husks off, and ate them (Luke 6:1–5). This by itself was not a problem: it was widely considered the right of hungry passersby to take a little food from the wayside. But they did this on a Sabbath, and were accused of doing unnecessary farm labor, "harvesting" on the holy day. Jesus reminded them of David, who took holy bread from the tabernacle for himself and his followers as they fled Saul (1 Sam. 21:1–6). If David did this and wasn't guilty of a sin, then the life-giving Sabbath was certainly a day when hungry people could pick a granola bar's worth of barley from the side of the road. Especially because, as he added, "The Son of Man is lord of the Sabbath" (Luke 6:5).

Luke records that the strict Pharisees were trying to catch Jesus breaking the Sabbath, and particularly looking for him to heal non-emergency maladies on that day. Jesus publicly addressed them: "I ask you, is it lawful on the Sabbath to do good or to do harm, to save life or to destroy it?" Not receiving an answer, he told the man to stretch out his hand. "And he did so, and his hand was restored" (Luke 6:9–10).

In the kingdom, the sick are healed, so Jesus healed the sick, *especially* on the Sabbath. He was, after all, preaching "the year of the Lord's favor"—the time of blessing to which all those missed Sabbath years pointed (Luke 4:19; Isa. 61:2). Mark's account of the grain-plucking argument includes these words of Jesus: "The Sabbath was made for man, not man for the Sabbath" (Mark 2:27). Just as he looked back to Adam and Eve in order to explain the lifelong nature of marriage, Jesus remembered that the Sabbath is not an occasion for prolonging misery or displaying how strict our righteousness can be: it's a gift from God, intended to relieve human suffering.

Much more can be said about the teaching of Jesus and how the early church put it into practice. We will get to these later, especially in the chapters on Worship and Rest. For now it's important to see that, far from ditching the Sabbath as many Christians do today, or "spiritualizing" it into something purely internal and personal, Jesus practiced it more seriously than his opponents, because his practice was in keeping with the meaning of the day. It was not a day to judge others for not keeping a labyrinth of rules: it was a day for showing mercy, feasting (even the minor feast of a handful of grain), healing, taking rest, and giving it to others.

4
OUR WORLD, WORK, AND FREEDOM

EVERY YEAR TOURO SYNAGOGUE in Newport, Rhode Island, reads aloud a letter from President George Washington written in 1790 thanking them for their welcome when he visited the city.

> The reflection on the days of difficulty and danger which are past is rendered the more sweet, from a consciousness that they are succeeded by days of uncommon prosperity and security. If we have wisdom to make the best use of the advantages with which we are now favored, we cannot fail, under the just administration of a good Government, to become a great and a happy people. . . . May the

> Children of the Stock of Abraham, who dwell in this land, continue to merit and enjoy the good will of the other Inhabitants; while every one shall sit in safety under his own vine and figtree, and there shall be none to make him afraid.

This friendly wish of the president is a *shalom* vision, a Sabbath vision, found in Deuteronomy, 1 and 2 Kings, Isaiah, Micah, and Zechariah: rest, independence, blessing, enjoying shade, food, and drink in one's own piece of the earth. It's an earthly vision of eternity. In it, the rest that God promises is not just ceasing from work, but enjoying the fruit of our work. More importantly, it is the enjoyment of God's blessing on us, poured out through (and sometimes in spite of) our work.

But we have built a world, not of *shalom*, but of restless coveting. The ways of Egypt (or Babel, or Israel at its worst) are alive and well among modern people. We too have powerful central governments with close ties to ultrarich elites. Our wealth comes not from the earth, but from trade—a global market of goods, delicately balanced and easily disrupted. Increasingly, we live in a rental economy, renting our books and movies and transportation. Even though countries such as the United States treat home ownership as a wonderful thing, most Americans don't really *own* their homes: they have mortgages, and if they stop paying, the bank will take possession and send them packing.

We live in a sophisticated, technological society—a society of planning and engineering. This definitely has its blessings: advances in tools and methods of medicine, communication, and transportation can save and enrich our lives. It also brings a degree of complexity that can make people lose their minds (literally), a rising inequality that gives most people less and less control over their own lives and unending covetousness. Absolutely everything around us is built to sell us more products. Cars, dishwashers, phones, and even buildings are designed to be out-of-date and unrepairable within months or years. They have more features and can "save energy" by some measures, allowing those who sell them to label them as environmentally friendly. But they are nearly impossible for an amateur to repair, leading either to expensive service calls or the purchase of newer models when they break (as they inevitably do).

We are not usually driven by material poverty (in the modern world few people go without plenty of food, adequate clothing, and some kind of shelter) but by an ever-changing array of "needs"—for a beautiful, new kitchen, a fearsome-looking truck, sub-10% body fat, respect in our career fields, etc. We view ourselves and our lives as things we create and achieve. For most of us, that means constant confusion and restlessness about *who we are* and *who we should be.* So we stare at, read about, work for, and lie awake thinking about this or that icon: the kitchen, the truck, the abs, the corner office. This, I think, is our idol worship. We literally serve images. Further, many use social media to "crowdsource" themselves: get a photo of yourself looking just so, say something funny, wise, woke, patriotic, etc., and post it. See if the right people like it (and the people you don't like hate it). See if it gets the views, likes, or clicks. Adjust as needed until it does.

In this way, the internet supercharges our discontent. We are literally not built to handle the fire hose of images that the internet sprays at us. Most human beings in history only ever saw hundreds or maybe a few thousand people in their whole lives. Now you can easily see thousands of people (or kitchens, or trucks) in an afternoon's browsing, and your emotions can't tell the difference between a high-resolution image and the real thing. How is anyone supposed to *not* covet their neighbor's house, wife, business, or ride?

The Sabbath speaks to a world wrapped up in work, worry, borrowing, lending, slaving, and taking. In any age, the world is full of those things. But we have become masters of them, using our sophisticated tools to create a sophisticated world that forgets God. We are not just sinners, we are *professional* sinners.

SABBATH AND BABEL

It makes sense to be impressed by human achievements. I'm particularly impressed by the accomplishments of ancient peoples: Polynesian sailors who crossed the Pacific, reliably navigating by the stars; Roman water and sewage systems that wouldn't be matched until well into the nineteenth century; or the Antikythera mechanism, a 2,000-year-old astronomical clock designed by an unknown Greek scientist.

In his book *1491,* Charles Mann describes artificial islands of compost on foundations of broken pottery, built by an unknown civilization in the middle of the soaking wet (but almost impossible to farm) Amazon River basin. Many hundreds of years later, locals get excited when they find mounds of "black earth" to till: the work of these unknown engineers grows the best crops in the basin. Fruit trees that were thought to be "native" to the Amazon were actually planted intentionally many lifetimes ago. To me, this is cooler than modern Dubai or Tokyo!

But whether you are impressed with the old or the new, the Eastern or the Western, farming or building, war or art, Sabbath is a time when we stop gazing with wonder at human achievement, stop achieving, enjoy what God has given to us (little or much), and praise him for his great works. Rabbi Abraham Joshua Heschel, reflecting on the Sabbath in the Jewish religion, wrestled with how to think about human accomplishment:

> The solution to mankind's most vexing problem will not be found in renouncing technical civilization,

but in attaining some degree of independence of it. In regard to external gifts, to outward possessions, there is only one proper attitude—to have them and to be able to do without them. On the Sabbath we live, as it were, *independent of technical civilization:* we abstain primarily from any activity that aims at remaking or reshaping the things of space. Man's royal privilege to conquer nature is suspended on the seventh day. (emphasis original)

Heschel is tackling a huge question. Technology and modern civilization have already changed human life radically from what our ancestors knew. Phones, cars, birth control, gene editing, and other inventions aren't just tools we use; they change us. How do we deal with that change? Just accept it? Become terrorists? Become Amish? Heschel suggests a better route: minimize the use of modern technology, at least once a week. We'll discuss what that looks like more in the second half of the book.

The book of Genesis records the attempt of an earlier civilization to rival God with their building and accomplishment. "Come, let us build ourselves a city and a tower with its top in the heavens, and let us make a name for ourselves, lest we be dispersed over the face of the whole earth" (Gen. 11:4). While the tower was pointed at heaven, those who built it hungered for unshakeable fame, power, and longevity on earth: eternal life. After he "came down" to see the city and tower, God sabotaged their efforts by confusing their language so that they could not understand one another. There is a lot to learn from the story of Babel. Here are two lessons: First, human beings have a powerful, sinful tendency to turn their work and accomplishments into weapons to challenge God and conquer their own limitations. Second, God will not have it.

The Sabbath is God's weekly answer to the Tower of Babel. We build ever bigger, ever more impressive things. That human urge to build and accomplish can be used to honor God, or it can be used to defy him (as at Babel). On the Sabbath we set aside our regular work. On the Sabbath we obey the psalmist's call to "Be still, and know that I am God." This is not a call to quiet reflection, but to stand at attention before the Lord: "I will be exalted among the nations, I will be exalted in the earth!" (Ps. 46:10). We accept his judgment and receive his instruction. He is King, not us.

The disciples of Jesus, looking at Herod's rebuilt temple (a wonder of the ancient world), said to him, "Teacher, what wonderful stones and what wonderful buildings!" Jesus told them not to be too impressed: "Do you see these great buildings? There will not be left here one stone upon another that will not be thrown down" (Mark 13:1–2). The Sabbath gives us perspective on the advanced civilization we live in: *This will all pass. God and his kingdom will not.*

A DIFFERENT WAY TO WORK

The Sabbath warns us against sinfully making our works into idols. The Sabbath is also rehab for the damage done by sin. We have been crippled in our ways of working, and our motives for work. We need to learn to walk again. We do not have to live the life of Babel. Work does not have to be about restless coveting. It can be an imitation of God (who is complete and needs nothing). We imitate God in our work through diligence, creativity, and patience.

Work is not life, and it is not our Lord. Early rising and long hours will not save us (Ps. 127:1–2). This may help us accomplish some short-term goals. But in the long term, self-salvation and self-invention both fail. It's been said that we tend to make a "good thing" into a "god thing"—we worship God's gifts as if they were gods.

Idol worshipers can't really enjoy the good things they are worshiping, and those who work without ceasing take all the joy out of work. Ultimately, they arrive at the conclusion Ecclesiastes did: "Vanity of vanities! All is vanity!" (Eccl. 1:2). Work is intended to be something other than self-salvation or self-invention. It's a way that we imitate God, the counterpart to imitating him in rest. That imitation takes three forms.

First, we imitate God in work through diligence. He did each day's distinct work and "saw that it was good." There is no task so little or lowly that we cannot glorify God by doing it attentively and thoroughly. Raking leaves for your parents or cleaning out the grease trap at Burger King? Be the best leaf-raker and grease trap–emptier they have ever seen. *All* work can be an act of worship; all work can be worth doing: "In all toil there is profit, but mere talk tends only to poverty" (Prov. 14:23).

Second, we imitate God in work through creativity. God's creativity was ultimate: he made all things *ex nihilo*, out of nothing, by speaking them into being. Our creativity is a stream spilling from his river. Creativity is different from diligence and discipline, but it is not their enemy. It lives at the edge of any kind of work, always saying, "I wonder if this could be done a different way"—a way that is more straightforward, easier, more interesting, more enjoyable, more beautiful, more effective. Creativity is full of ideas, and most of them fail. Any field of work needs both diligence and creativity. Without diligence, nothing gets done. Without creativity, nothing gets better.

Third, we imitate God in work through patience. For human beings, it is impossible to tell which of our projects and plans will succeed before we begin them. Some fall apart immediately. Others go on for hours, months, years, or decades before we see them falter—or flourish. This is true of work, relationships, home life, and church health and growth. Our careers may be spectacular or disastrous: it takes time to find out. Our projects may be worthwhile or a waste of time. God does not wonder about the future, but he is patient. He does not "cancel the project" of human lives, nations, or civilizations quickly. He grants time for repentance (or else hardening in our sin), for growth (or else shrinking into ourselves), for flourishing (or for our rebellious souls to sicken and die).

For many of us, the need for patience is clearest in our childrearing. We go through the labor and bearing of children, then the expense, care, and mixed joy-and-sorrow of raising them. Sometimes they die young (grief of griefs), sometimes they struggle with troubles of their own in life—sin or illness or addiction or immaturity—and sometimes they turn out to be scoundrels. But surprisingly often, they grow and flourish and bear good fruit in the world, bringing joy and honor to their parents and communities (Prov. 23:22–25). This is the grace of God, and God is teaching us patience as we wonder, weep, and wait to see what happens.

There is no guarantee that if we work hard we will enjoy the fruit of our labor—all the diligence, creativity, and patience in the world can do nothing without the blessing of the Creator. The Sabbath day teaches us that we need God's blessing on our work. Our work is crowned and blessed when we can set our work aside and enjoy its fruits. Our work is cursed if there are no fruits to enjoy or no time to enjoy them. My friend Sammy, who came to America from Burundi (sometimes ranked the poorest country in the world), joked, "In America we have a couch and no time to sit on it."

The right way to approach work, then, is to worship God by imitating him in work and rest. This is the only real alternative to the restless coveting of the world.

WORK, SABBATH, AND SACRIFICE

Work was a reality in the garden of Eden, but it was easy and fruitful. Sin changed that. God said to Adam, "By the sweat of your face you shall eat bread, till you return to the ground, for out of it you were taken; for you are dust, and to dust you shall return" (Gen. 3:19). Adam's sons, Cain and Abel, were both farmers, and both offered the produce of their work to God.

> Now Abel was a keeper of sheep, and Cain a worker of the ground. In the course of time Cain brought to the LORD an offering of the fruit of the ground, and Abel also brought of the firstborn of his flock and of their fat portions. And the LORD had regard for Abel and his offering, but for Cain and his offering he had no regard. So Cain was very angry, and his face fell. (Gen. 4:2–5)

This passage is deep water, and it makes us ask deep questions. First, how did they know whether their offerings were acceptable? Most likely, Abel's work was blessed and flourished, while Cain's was not. Second, what was the problem with Cain's offering? Was it that God preferred sheep to grain? Possibly. But more likely, Cain's heart was not right before God: "Why are you angry? And why is your face gloomy?" the Lord asks him. "If you do well, will your face not be cheerful? And if you do not do well, sin is lurking at the door; and its desire is for you, but you must master it" (Gen. 4:6–7 NASB).

You cannot get away from sacrifices and offerings in the Bible. David must have been thinking about the anger of Cain when he wrote, "Be angry, and do not sin; ponder in your own hearts on your beds, and be silent. Offer right sacrifices, and put your trust in the LORD" (Ps. 4:4–5). Old Testament sacrifices of sheep, grain, goats, pigeons, wine, oil, and oxen brought messages to God, underlining the prayers of the people: "I praise you! Provide us with food! Thank you for giving us victory in war! Bless this child! Thank you for the harvest! Forgive my sins!"

We may think of the Old Covenant as more interested in earthly blessings than the new, but the first "personal" petition of the great New Covenant prayer is, "Give us this day our daily bread." In every time, human beings, who have bodies and live in a world full of danger and possibility, need God to provide and protect, as well as forgive. Work and Sabbath rest are offerings by which we ask God to prosper and provide for us, and thank him for answering those prayers.

Talking about sacrifice might seem strange in a Christian book. Most of the time we talk about "sacrifice" loosely, as in "I had to sacrifice a lot to afford this boat," or else we talk about it as something that Christ did so we don't have to. But the angel appears to Cornelius and says, "Your prayers and alms have ascended as a memorial before God" (Acts 10:4). The language is of an Old Testament *memorial-offering* (Lev. 24:7). Cornelius had made the only offerings he lawfully could as a Gentile—prayers and gifts to the poor—and God had heard him.

Later the writer of Hebrews tells his readers to offer God two sacrifices in worship: "Through [Jesus] then let us continually offer up a sacrifice of praise to God, that is, the fruit of lips that acknowledge his name. Do not neglect to do good and to share what you have, for such sacrifices are pleasing to God" (Heb. 3:15–16). In other words, we *are* to sacrifice to God, in order to praise and please him.

Our sacrifices of generosity, praise, and other obedience are not merits in the Roman Catholic sense. We do not score points with God, earning either eternal life or earthly blessings. How could we, if everything we have is a gift from him? We cannot put God in our debt, because he needs nothing from us. The same thing could be said of spiritual disciplines like prayer and fasting. I cannot tell Almighty God anything he doesn't already know, and I cannot force him to do anything by depriving myself of food.

Nonetheless, the offerings of prayer, alms, fasting, work, and Sabbath *do* please God, and they tell him that we are serious about our needs and desires. He loves to give good gifts to his children, and he likes to be asked, because our asking and thanking him brings him glory. When it comes down to it, *every* kind of obedience is sacrifice if it is costly. King David said, "I will not offer burnt offerings to the Lord my God that cost me nothing" (2 Sam. 24:24).

Working to the glory of God is a kind of sacrifice. So is resting in the time and way God commands. I may know I need to both work and rest, but my desires at a given moment don't always match that knowledge. When it's time to work, I feel like slacking off. When it's time to rest, I want to get going on my projects and tasks. But when I do what I should, regardless of my feelings at the moment, that's an offering to the living God, in hope of his blessing, all for the sake of Christ.

WHAT IF I'M A SLAVE?

Slavery is as old as humanity, and it is terrible. Details vary, but in all cases a slave is someone who works and rests at the will of another. A slave does not have a genuine option of walking away. This is true whether or not the slave makes a lot of money (there are examples of very wealthy slaves in the ancient world). It is true whether or not that person is treated well. The history of Israel in Egypt tells us that good treatment in slavery is temporary. First Pharaoh took land at the time the nation was willing to trade farms for emergency help. Then he took labor. Finally he took ownership of life itself (Exod. 1:15–22).

Free and independent people work their own little patch of the world for a profit or a harvest, not for a wage. A free person doesn't "have a job"; he takes on projects and responsibilities. He is not weighed down with debt and is not worried about the future, partly because he has been prudent in his planning, but much more because he trusts in God's care. A free person runs more risks: Pharaoh (or a nanny state or a giant corporation or a plantation owner) is always there to provide for the slave, but the free person depends on the grace of God and the kindness of neighbors in time of disaster.

People can be slaves whether or not they wear chains, and whether or not they live in grinding poverty. "The borrower is the slave of the lender" (Prov. 22:7). Well-paid personnel at staggeringly rich Wall Street firms talk about "golden handcuffs"—salaries, bonuses, and stock options so generous (and often vested in the future) that they can't bring themselves to walk away, especially after they've gotten used to a certain lifestyle.

What should you do if you are a slave or feel like one? Paul tackles the question in 1 Corinthians. First he advises

Christians to be content in whatever life situation they find themselves in. Then he tells them not to let it bother them if they are slaves, because they can still serve the Lord in slavery: "Were you a bondservant [slave] when called? Do not be concerned about it." Then he adds, "But if you can gain your freedom, avail yourself of the opportunity" (1 Cor. 7:21).

You can serve God in any situation: in slavery in Egypt, in slavery in ancient Rome, $200,000 in debt for a degree in social work, or as a vice president at Citi Private Bank, paying for your Manhattan mortgage. You may be in your situation because of your own decisions or through no fault of your own or through a mix of bad luck, bad guidance, and bad choices. Serve God where you are. "Bondservants, obey in everything those who are your earthly masters, not by way of eye-service, as people-pleasers, but with sincerity of heart, fearing the Lord" (Col. 3:22). "Let all who are under a yoke as bondservants regard their own masters as worthy of all honor, so that the name of God and the teaching may not be reviled" (1 Tim. 6:1). If you are a slave, work as for God, not as for man.

But: if you can, get your freedom. If you can get out of debt, gain some independence, get a patch of land and plant your own vine and fig tree, wisely start a little business (get good advice first!), do it. Two other passages always come to my mind when I think about this kind of freedom: "Owe no one anything, except to love each other, for the one who loves another has fulfilled the law" (Rom. 13:8). "But we urge you, brothers, . . . to aspire to live quietly, and to mind your own affairs, and to work with your hands, as we instructed you, so that you may walk properly before outsiders and be dependent on no one" (1 Thess. 4:10–12).

My wife and I moved from the urban neighborhood that we loved to a spacious (for Rhode Island) two-acre piece of old farmland. As we started eating the produce of our garden, Esther remarked: "Can you imagine how people felt every day of their lives, when everything they ate and wore and used was something they grew, or made, or built—or it was grown or made or built by someone they knew? Their lives must have been so *meaningful.*"

Maybe you will get rich (probably not). Maybe you will be more comfortable (probably not). But I dare say your life will be more full of meaning than ever. You will have more opportunity to serve the Lord, you'll be happier, and you'll be free.

But if you cannot get that freedom: be at peace. Freedom is coming.

5
PART 1 RECAP

IN ORDER TO UNDERSTAND the Sabbath, we first need to see it through the eyes of an ancient Israelite. That starts with understanding the life of Egypt from which Israel was freed in the exodus. Egypt was the great civilization of the known world. Pharaoh was worshiped as a god and had absolute control over his land and its inhabitants. Egyptian life was based around the annual flooding of the Nile River, which provided irrigation water and made farming on an enormous scale possible. Pharaoh used his wealth to build great monuments and store cities and he managed the Hebrews, as well as others, by enslaving and selectively controlling their population. Egypt was run by expert managers and engineers.

When God rescued his people from Egypt, he humbled Egypt's power and lifted up Egypt's slaves. Despite their servitude, Israel had grown and learned to farm from their captors. God told them not to practice the ways of Egypt: fearfulness, restlessness, love of riches, and idol worship. The Sabbath commandment was a perpetual reminder of this. They learned that there is only one true God and that he creates us and saves us as a gift of his grace. Because the world belongs to God, it does not work the way that Egypt thought it worked.

Israel was to live in their new land in keeping with God's grace. They were to enjoy God's gift of Sabbath rest and share it with others. They were not to crush poor workers. Everyone was to have the opportunity to work their land and provide for their own needs. Even debts would be periodically canceled. All of this was a refusal of Egypt's fear of the future and lust for power, and a testimony that even though we work to provide for ourselves, God provides for us.

The people of God were to avoid the arrogance and self-invention of the ancient empires. The world was not in their control, as they well knew. They were called to work diligently each week and trust God to bless that work, not attempt to be gods in his place, saving themselves and setting up rival kingdoms. And on the Sabbath they were called to rest. Sabbath rest is agreement with God that the world he made is very good.

Part 1 Recap

The Sabbath wasn't just an answer to the tyranny of Egypt and other foreign empires, it was a rebuke to privileged elites in Israel who robbed others of their freedom and self-reliance in order to enrich themselves further. The prophets of Israel repeatedly called for a genuine keeping of the Sabbath as part of repentance for idolatry, love of money, and immorality.

Following the Babylonian exile, the remnant of Israel got the message and took the Sabbath much more seriously. But this created the conditions for other problems, such as the hypocritical Sabbath keeping of the Pharisees. Multiple times Jesus was accused of doing unnecessary work or healing on the Sabbath. His response was both that his critics misunderstood the purpose of the Sabbath—which was supposed to be freeing and lifegiving—and that they didn't recognize his authority as Lord of the Sabbath.

Today we live in a society even more complex and advanced than ancient Egypt—a society driven by coveting (which, Paul said, "is idolatry" [Col. 3:5]). The Sabbath gives us a perspective on life in an advanced technological society: we are not to escape it at all costs, but we are to set it aside each week, stop being impressed with mankind, and be impressed with God. The Christian Sabbath teaches us the meaning of work in such a society: it is not a means of creating or saving ourselves, but a means of imitating God and waiting on him to provide for our needs. We can serve

God in any work situation, even slavery and situations that feel like slavery. But if we can become independent and free, we should.

PART 2: SABBATH HOW

6
WORSHIP

THE HEART OF OUR HOLY DAY is a holy gathering to meet with our holy God. The most central and basic way we are called to keep the Sabbath is to worship with the church.

There's a difference between taking a day off and celebrating the day. Even though I appreciate what American workers have done, I have never particularly *celebrated* Labor Day: I don't even know if there are parades or celebrations near me that I could attend. Usually I just think of it as a day off, the last one before school starts in the fall. I have gone to ceremonies or parades on Memorial Day, Veterans Day, and Independence Day, but not consistently. I have attended church services on Martin Luther King Day. On the other hand, I have never skipped Thanksgiving dinner. My sister's family sometimes has Thanksgiving dinner in the morning or at night because her husband has to work a day shift. My father once worked a double shift on Christmas Day (double time-and-a-half!), but we still found a way to open presents together. All of that to say: a day off is nice, but it's not the whole picture. A day off makes room for a celebration, and the celebration is the point.

Rooms and buildings are arranged around the most important things that happen in them. A well-designed kitchen has a "work triangle" of stove, sink, and refrigerator. Even a badly designed kitchen has those things somewhere in or near it. A church sanctuary focuses on the pulpit and communion table. You can cook without a kitchen, but not without heat. You can worship without a sanctuary, but not without Word and Sacrament. In the same way, the Sabbath is arranged around worship. It is a space designed to make worship possible.

The Bible teaches that we have been redeemed from sin and death in order to worship. For instance, the Lord told Pharaoh, "Let my people go, that they may serve me" (Exod. 8:1). Pharaoh understood that serving the Lord meant *worship:* "Plead with the Lord . . . and I will let the people go to sacrifice to the Lord" (Exod. 8:8). Later, when Israel was free of Egypt, chapters and chapters—whole books—were dedicated to regulations for tabernacle and temple worship. All of life is to be service to the Lord, and at the heart of all service is our service of gathered, focused worship.

Every year on Independence Day, American identity is at the front of Americans' minds, and we remember that this identity is more important than many others—city, state, political party, race, baseball team, favorite brand of car. In the same way, when Christians worship together on the Lord's Day, our Christian identity dwarfs all of the other things that *seem* important during the rest of the week.

If worship is so central to the Sabbath, why doesn't the fourth commandment mention worship? It's important to read the fourth commandment in the context of the first three, which are almost entirely focused on religious worship. First commandment: worship *only God.* Second commandment: worship God *only as he tells us to worship him.* Third commandment: *worship* (the most important way we "take up" the name of the Lord) *from the heart, genuinely,* not in an empty ("vain") manner. Those things prepare us for the fourth, which links together the God-focused first three with the neighbor-focused last six. Fourth commandment: *rest, and give others rest, making space for all to worship God.*

IS THE SABBATH FOR CHRISTIANS?

Many reject or question the idea that Christians are to take a day of rest. Some do this because they've simply never heard that the Sabbath is for Christians. Others interpret the

Bible as dropping the fourth commandment with the coming of Christ and the dawn of the New Testament church. There's a reason I've waited until now to tackle this question, rather than putting it in the "Sabbath Why" section of the book, and this will become clear in a little bit.

In Reformed theology, we often talk about God making "covenants" with human beings. That's how he relates to us. While God's grace is always part of one "covenant of grace," that big covenant is revealed in two phases: the Old Covenant given through Moses and the New Covenant given through Jesus. (These two roughly correspond to the Old and New Testaments in the Bible.)

While it's clearly not okay to throw out one of God's big Ten Commandments because it's inconvenient or foreign to us, the shift from one covenant to another brings up an important question: what does the law of Moses (and the Sabbath commandment in particular) have to do with Christians? The teachings of Jesus on the Sabbath do not answer the question as directly as we might like, because Jesus's ministry was almost entirely among Jews, in the ancient Jewish homeland, and most Christians are not Jewish. So although Jesus clearly did not suspend, cancel, or personally break the Sabbath (as he was accused of doing), it's reasonable to seek an answer to the question: what about the Gentiles?

In the book of Acts and the letters of the New Testament, we see the good news of Christ going to many nations, as

Christ commanded (Matt. 28:19–20; Acts 1:8). His disciples began their witness in Jerusalem, but went from there through Judea and Samaria (the ancient kingdom of David) and far beyond. The first hearers and believers of the gospel in almost every city were Jewish. Paul and other missionaries went first to the synagogues, where people worshiped the one true God, believed that the Hebrew Bible was his Word, and were waiting for the Messiah. But as time went on, the conversions took place more and more among Gentile (non-Jewish) people. At a certain point, math took over: there were and are vastly more non-Jews than Jews, and by the end of the first century AD, Gentiles made up the majority of Christians.

The New Testament records early Jewish Christians continuing to gather in the temple and synagogues on the seventh day. This is because the New Testament (especially before the destruction of ancient Jerusalem in the Jewish War of 66–70) was a time of overlap for Jewish Christians. The practices and institutions of ancient Judaism remained in place for a time. So what did *Gentile* Christians do? Is there evidence that they kept a Sabbath on the seventh day or any other?

Yes. In the New Testament, the Christian Sabbath can be seen in the church's worship on the first day of the week. In the days following Jesus's resurrection, his disciples began the distinctly Christian practice of gathering for worship on the first day—an indication that while the Sabbath continued, the day of its observance had changed. Just as the seventh-day Sabbath celebrated the beginning of the world, the first-day Sabbath celebrated the beginning of a new world under the reign of the Lord Jesus.

Ancient worship was simple. The church gathered (usually in homes), celebrated communion, read and received teaching from Scripture, prayed, sang psalms, and collected food and money for the care of the poor and for the support of their leaders. And from the day of Jesus's resurrection on, it took place on the first day of the week, which John the apostle calls "the Lord's Day" in Revelation (Rev. 1:10). Jesus appeared to his disciples when they were gathered on the first day (John 20:19) and broke bread with them (Luke 24:30). In the mixed Jewish–Gentile churches that Paul planted or preached in, gatherings "to break bread" clearly took place on the first day of the week (Acts 20:7; 1 Cor. 10:16 with 16:2). Paul's instructions on putting together an offering for the poor make it clear that the church in Corinth gathered regularly and normally for worship on the first day (1 Cor. 16:2)—and that generous giving was part of worship.

First-day worship was immediately normal, even mandatory. But there is no mention in the New Testament of first-day rest. There is very little in Christian writings of the first few centuries. While we shouldn't build too much on an "argument from silence," this silence is loud. It seems that most Christians did not take Sunday as a day of rest, and we who believe in a Christian Sabbath owe skeptics an explanation. (After all, while we are in the majority among Christians throughout history, we are in the minority among Protestants today.)

Why didn't they rest? They couldn't, for several reasons. The Jews were a well-known and vocal minority in the Roman Empire, and many (including the family of Herod the Great) were closely tied to emperors and other powerful people. This gained them some important legal privileges, such as paying a tax to support the Jerusalem temple, instead of directly to the empire, and being allowed to rest on their weekly Sabbath. The Jewish Sabbath had wide legal recognition. Early Christians had no such legal protection, and wouldn't for centuries.

As far as the Romans were concerned, they were a sect of the Jews: the Roman writer Suetonius wrote that "the Jews constantly made disturbances at the instigation of Chrestus," leading Emperor Claudius to expel them from Rome (see Acts 18:2). It's very possible that this was trouble between Christian and non-Christian Jews over "Chrestus" (or "Christus"). From a pagan official's perspective, there was no difference at this point: just a bunch of Jews having arguments with each other. As the proconsul Gallio sneered, "It is a matter of questions about words and names and your own law" (Acts 18:15). Christians were only beginning to be recognized by the empire as a separate group, and only in some places (Acts 11:26).

So there was no possibility of widespread legal protection for Christians who wished to rest on the first day of the week. No doubt, wealthy and powerful people could take a day of rest when they saw fit, but not many Christians fit this description (1 Cor. 1:26). Many of them were slaves (1 Cor. 7:21–23; 1 Tim. 6:1), with essentially zero control over their own schedules. It would not be until the 300s AD that Emperor Constantine would make Sunday (literally Sun Day) a legal holiday. This was openly a day in honor of the Unconquered Sun, a popular deity among Roman soldiers (see the movie *Gladiator*), but it was probably intended by Constantine as a cover for Christians who wanted to rest and worship in honor of the resurrected Christ.

One common theme among ancient Christian writings on the Sabbath is that Jesus brings to the world the true rest promised by the Old Testament Sabbath. Theologian Augustine of Hippo (354–430) wrote,

> So, when you ask why a Christian does not keep the Sabbath, if Christ came not to destroy the law, but to fulfill it, my reply is, that a Christian does not keep the Sabbath precisely because what was prefigured in the Sabbath is fulfilled in Christ. For we have our

> Sabbath in Him who said, "Come unto me, all ye that labor and are heavy laden, and I will give you rest. Take my yoke upon you, and learn of me; for I am meek and lowly in heart, and ye shall find rest unto your souls."

The ancients were unified in seeing Jesus as the fulfillment of the Old Testament stories and images. Jesus is the bread of life—the manna Israel ate was a picture of him. Jesus gives the water of life: the rock that Moses struck is a picture of him. Jesus is the giver of rest: the Sabbath Moses taught is a picture of him. Does this mean that we only eat and drink and rest "spiritually"? Of course not. We still take communion and get baptized and rest on the Lord's Day *as we are able.*

Any believer given Sunday off would have rejoiced to honor the Lord by resting as well as worshiping. Even before Constantine, Christians understood that the first day was *the Lord's Day* and a day of rejoicing. The *Epistle of Barnabas* (c. 100) speaks of a coming eternal Sabbath in much the same way Hebrews does (Heb. 4:1–13). But it goes on to reason that since God will one day bring about this eternal "eighth day," "therefore we keep the eighth day with joyfulness, the day also on which Jesus rose from the dead." Tertullian (c. 155–220) spoke of the Lord's Day as a day of joy and festivity in *De Corona* and *Ad Nationes*.

In 360, the Council of Laodicea made a ruling that fits particularly well with the message of this chapter: "Christians must not judaize by resting on the [seventh day], but must work on that day, rather honouring the Lord's Day; and, if they can, resting then as Christians" (Canon XXIX). The church leaders gathering in Laodicea were describing a clear shift, from a seventh-day rest to a first-day rest, encouraging Christians to make this their Sabbath, "if they can." (Good news: to one extent or another, almost everyone can!)

Worship is the indispensable part of our Sabbath keeping. Without worship we cannot say we are keeping the Sabbath or the fourth commandment, even if we get the practices described in following chapters right. Israel could not rest in Egypt, and Christians cannot rest in hostile places and times. But ancient believers—slave and free, rich and poor—went to church. Often they had to steal through the darkness of early morning or evening to worship in an unmarked house. They ran risks to worship with God's people. And so should we.

The ancient church's experience matters more than ever. We are seeing our culture's respect for the Sabbath erode at a remarkable pace. But we should not assume that even Western countries with a background of Christian faith have historically respected the Lord's Day. Historian Joseph S. Moore writes that "the United States is a more Christian nation today than it was when the Founders wrote the Constitution." He goes on to elaborate:

> We trust God on our coins (1864) and paper money (1955). The Post Office no longer opens on Sunday (1912). Students pledge allegiance to a nation "under God" (1954) and spend government loans and grants to study theology at religious schools (1944, 1965). An entire government office focuses on helping religious charities use tax money (2001). Presidents Bush and Obama both called for national days of prayer each year they were in office, something President Jefferson refused to do and President Madison did once but later regretted.

Religious freedoms have not always existed, and we cannot take them for granted. The legal right to rest on the Sabbath is one example. It was hard won, in the United States at least. Certainly it was hard won for Israel! Use it or lose it.

WHY WE WORSHIP

God is our Maker. He is the source of all blessing. Above all, he is the source of salvation. These are enough reasons to worship him. But most people (including me) are not persuaded to do something unless they see that it is good *for themselves.* Let's take a minute to talk about why we need to worship.

God does not need our worship. "Every beast of the forest is mine, the cattle on a thousand hills," God says in Psalm 50. "If I were hungry, I would not tell you, for the world and its fullness are mine" (Ps. 50:10, 12). When we praise him, we add nothing to his praise. All glory belongs to him.

But we owe God our praise, and we have a basic need to worship him. Human beings can't help being worshipers. We are not so much "rational animals" (Aristotle's definition of mankind) as worshiping animals. We find something beautiful and gather around it in wonder and adoration: cheer it at parades, watch it on TV, risk our lives to protect it, buy the T-shirt. Either we will worship and adore what is highest and best (the Creator himself) or we will worship something lower. *Worship is inevitable.* If we do not worship the true God, we will worship some sort of idol.

Christian worship is a gathering of God's people to meet with him. Yes, there is individual worship ("devotions") and family worship, but "corporate" (congregational) worship is the priority for us. Individual and family spirituality flow from corporate worship, not the other way around.

In Reformed theology we sometimes talk about the "visible" and "invisible" church. The visible church is the flesh-and-blood institution that is expressed in local churches and denominations, with all of its flaws. The invisible church is the eternal Bride of Christ, everywhere in all time. Few people use these terms today, but the concepts are important. Ignorant people think that they can maintain a Christian identity while keeping their distance from flesh-and-blood churches (after all, I'm a busy person, and besides, churches are full of hypocrites!). But if you are alive and on earth, the way to be a Christian (part of the invisible church) is to be part of a worshiping body of believers (part of the visible church). It is "the house and family of God, out of which there is no ordinary possibility of salvation," says the *Westminster Confession*. In short, while going to church doesn't make you a Christian, living as a Christian requires going to church.

You cannot sing psalms without feeling the burning desire of the psalmists for *gathering* with God's people: "These things I remember, as I pour out my soul: how I would go with the throng and lead them in procession to the house of God with glad shouts and songs of praise, a multitude keeping festival" (Ps. 42:4). This is an image of heaven, and corporate worship prepares us for heaven. Much of what we read about heaven makes it sound like a hot, noisy party. (That's a good time for some of us, but not for all of us. I think J. R. R. Tolkien was probably thinking of heaven when he wrote this description of the Last Homely House: "Rivendell was the perfect house, whether you liked food or story-telling or singing, or just sitting and thinking best, or a pleasant mixture of them all. Merely to be there was a cure for weariness, fear and sadness." Other scriptural images show us the other sides of heaven: green pastures, dew-drenched mountains, the smaller-scale joy of the family table, the sleep of peace, the vine and the fig tree.)

There's no room in this book for a full-blown discussion of worship. But church worship—as plain and humble as it is in the Presbyterian tradition—is a table that God has set for us and is full of good things: strength for the weak, instruction for the ignorant, conviction for those in sin, assurance for the miserable, forgiveness for the repentant, and healing for the damaged. Sometimes we avoid worship because we don't think we need these things. But if we don't eat the meal God has set for us, our hunger will not go away, and we will seek to have our spiritual needs met somewhere else. As a pastor I have come to see this: skipping church is a check engine light, an indicator of other sin issues, either now or soon.

Worship makes us a people: it defines the church. You do not deserve the name Christian because you "identify" as one or vote a certain way. You deserve the name because you gather with a Christian body (though not all who go to worship will prove to belong to Christ). The Hebrew term for Israel at worship is *qahal*, gathering or assembly. The Greek word usually translated "church" is *ekklēsia*, literally "those called out," meaning that we have been called out of wherever we are from to become a new people. Augustine, in *City of God*, defined a people as "a gathered multitude of rational beings united by agreeing to share the things they love." We may start out as extremely different people, even as enemies. But loving something and sharing it makes us a people.

What should we think of Christians who do not go to church? What we think of families who never eat or spend time together and couples who never share a bed. It's not so much that coming together in these ways strengthens the bond (as if the bond was "spiritual" and had nothing to do with bodies). It's more that these *are* the bonds.

The church unites souls and bodies around the crucified and risen Christ to share in him through the Word and Sacraments. Physical separation weakens the unity of souls. When we gather, we minister to each other. We teach and "admonish *one another*" to persevere in faith and obedience by singing "psalms, hymns, and spiritual songs" (Eph. 5:17; Col. 3:16). Singing praise isn't a solo sport. Just as nations celebrate independence or victory in war, we weekly celebrate the resurrection, the moment when salvation came into the world, especially for those who believe (1 Tim. 4:10). Christians can disagree about other holidays, but there should be no disagreement about our weekly holy day.

The world is schizophrenic about bodies. Abortion advocates shout, "My body, my choice!" (achieving the extermination of other people's children) and many people (even many Christians) think that "consenting adults" should be allowed to do whatever they want with each other. But is this really a love or appreciation of the body? If I set my car on fire, because it's my car and I want to watch it burn, does that express love or respect for God's gift of that car? Sexual freedom has reached an extreme, almost pre-Christian pitch. But the kids these days aren't having as much sex as their parents did in the '70s and '80s, according to journalist Kate Julian in *The Atlantic Monthly*. We exalt our bodies and their pleasures, then we treat them like playthings, then we lose them.

Almost all of life now comes through a screen. Why can't church? Internet church, like internet sex, is safe, voyeuristic, sterile, sedative, and eventually deadly. In times of emergency, we may have to "go to church" online, but don't do it for long. People play games on their phone that mimic farming or raising children. Is this *real* farming and child-rearing? Is it *better* than the old-fashioned ways? Is any real food grown; are any real children nurtured? *Real* religion requires an embodied worship, not a disembodied one. Consider the second commandment: "You shall not *make* for yourself a carved image. . . . You shall not *bow down* to them or *serve* them." Paul says that our *spiritual* worship is to present our *bodies* as a living sacrifice to God (Rom. 12:1). James says, "I will show you my faith by my works" (James 2:18). We worship with our bodies as well as our hearts. They are inseparable.

We gather in the flesh because Jesus came to us in the flesh. Entire heresies have been built around the idea that the incarnation was a mistake, somehow beneath God's dignity. But "the Word became flesh and dwelt among us" (John 1:14). In his letters John underlines this: "By this you know the Spirit of God: every spirit that confesses that Jesus Christ has come in the flesh is from God" (1 John 4:2).

The advent of the train and the car transformed church. You could now ride or drive past thousands of neighbors and dozens of churches to attend the one of your preference. You might never see another member of your church from one Sunday morning until the next. The advent of internet church threatens to destroy church altogether. With high-quality audio and video, we can have high-budget, high-production-quality church services—usually showcasing a compelling preacher—without leaving home. It sure feels better than going to the community church three blocks away, with its aluminum siding and lame praise banners. And it might feel better than driving an hour to attend a church you agree with theologically.

Maybe what we are trying to escape by staying home from church (whether or not we use the internet as a substitute) is not the weak preaching, the off-key singing, or the shabby facility. Maybe it's the people. We just don't want to deal with the people we find in church: don't want to open our lives to them, don't want to help them with their problems. Everyone has a certain capacity for friendships, and maybe we feel our capacity is nearly full.

Of course, some people choose to skip church, not for internet worship, but for time in nature. At least time in nature is healthy! Can you meet God in nature? Certainly, especially if you go off a cliff while mountain biking or drown while surfing. Is spending time in the woods or the mountains or on the water good for your soul? Dark humor aside, yes. It's hard to overestimate *how* good it is for your body and your soul. But that is not the most beautiful and transformative part of God's creation:

> When I consider Your heavens, the work of Your
> > fingers,
> > The moon and the stars, which You have set in
> > > place;
> > What is man that You think of him,
> > > And the son of man that You are concerned
> > > > about him?
> > Yet You have made him a little lower than God,
> > > And You crown him with glory and majesty!
> (Ps. 8:3–5 NASB)

As beautiful as you may find a mountain range or ocean, God looks at a crowded subway car and finds it more beautiful. And the church is even more lovely in the eyes of her Savior. God looks at those not-glamorous, not-fascinating, not-put-together people in the pews and sees them "beautiful as the moon, bright as the sun, awesome as an army with banners" (Song of Sol. 6:10).

GO TO CHURCH

Put the kayak back in the garage, turn off the computer, and go to church. Commit and submit to a congregation, a worshiping body. I suggest a solid Reformed church (ideally in my denomination!), but it's better to be a faithful and involved member in a tolerable church than to travel a crazy distance to an amazing church. There is no perfect church, and if you found it, you would spoil it by joining it. Humble yourself to be with the humble: God does (Isa. 57:15).

Worship is our most basic act of Sabbath keeping—the thing we do even when we can't do anything else. Get enough sleep on Saturday night. Prepare clothes and food the night before, because the devil likes Sunday morning domestic chaos. Families, especially, need to get moving faster than they generally think: shoot for getting to church fifteen minutes early and you *might* get there on time. (It's amazing how many diaper blowouts or arguments over hair care happen on Sunday morning.)

And what if your job *won't let you* go to worship? Then, my friend, you are in a near-emergency situation and should do whatever you can to get out of it. Talk to your elders about getting a letter explaining your religion's requirement that you attend worship services regularly (more about this in the Rest chapter and in Appendix 2). You may not get your way. Keep your eyes open for a different job. Most important: pray, and ask your church to pray. The power of prayer is greater than the power of power.

7
FEASTING

THE WORD *PARADISE* comes from the Greek for "garden." The garden of Eden was, literally, paradise: a place of pleasure and leisure. There Adam and Eve enjoyed God's rich provision for them: "every tree that is pleasant to the sight and good for food" (Gen. 2:9). They had not planted or raised up the garden, nor had they done anything to deserve being there. They were just *there.* Even better, they had unbroken, unstained fellowship with their Creator. When Jesus said to the thief on the cross, "Today you will be with me in paradise" (Luke 23:43), he meant heaven, because in the presence of God there is joy, pleasure, abundance, and rest (Ps. 16:11).

But we know how the story continues. The first man and woman were thrown from paradise for their sin: worst of all, they were cut off from the fellowship of God. Cherubim and a flaming sword kept them from returning. The ancient tabernacle and temple were built to be models of Eden, and embroidered cherubim covered the veil between the Holy Place and the Most Holy Place. Just as the presence of God in the garden was forbidden for sinful man, so was the presence of God in the Most Holy Place. Man was also cut off from the abundance of the garden. For the rest of human history, mankind would eat bread by the sweat of his face (Gen. 3:19). Food would be gained by backbreaking labor, it would often be scanty, and it would always be uncertain.

The salvation of Jesus Christ restores both the presence of God and his blessing. At the moment of Jesus's death the temple veil was torn in two from top to bottom (Matt. 27:51). Offering himself up as an atonement for sin, Jesus brings us back into the presence of God "by the new and living way that he opened for us" (Heb. 10:20). In Jesus, we who were far are brought near (Eph. 2:13, 17). When we meet Jesus we meet God (John 14:9).

Being restored to the presence of God that we lost in Eden, we are also promised the provision of God that we lost in Eden. God promises to provide for our needs. That is what we expect in eternity: the "marriage supper of the Lamb" (Rev. 19:9), a table that God sets for us, a feast we did not cook, let alone earn. The kingdom of God is not just something we will know about or see, it is something we will *enjoy.* We are promised a feast. We live in expectation of this promise, in several ways.

We remember Christ's promise whenever we celebrate the Lord's Supper (Communion) in worship. The simple sharing of bread and a cup looks back at the past and ahead to the future. The "living bread that came down from heaven" has been shared with us, once and for all (John 6:51). When we take Communion, we eat that bread again, in expectation that we will "live forever" (v. 58). We feast to celebrate Christ, whose "flesh is true food" and "blood is true drink" (v. 55).

We remember Christ's promise of coming joy when we *rest*, as we will see in the next chapter. The burden of responsibility to change and transform the world and to provide for ourselves and others is set aside for a day. We testify that in Christ, "he has done it," not us (Ps. 22:31). And we anticipate the coming Sabbath rest that remains for the people of God (Heb. 4:9–10).

As we will see in chapter 9, we remember Christ's promise when we share with those in need. The generosity of the early church took various forms in different places, but the principle is the same everywhere: everyone gets enough. Rich people in Jerusalem sold off properties and gave the proceeds to the apostles so that the poorest believers would have their daily bread (Acts 2:44–45; 4:32–37). Christians in areas unaffected by a famine in Judea shared generously with their brothers in Jerusalem so that there would be "fairness" (2 Cor. 8:13–14). God's economy is one of abundance. When you have the riches of heaven in your hands and in your future, you can afford to be generous.

In this chapter we will look at living in light of the coming kingdom by *feasting*, particularly feasting on the Lord's Day. "Feasting" might sound a bit foreign, a bit medieval (picture court jesters and turkey legs), and certainly not *healthy*. You might talk about going to a "dinner," a "barbecue," or a "party," but "feast" seems like it must be too much of a good thing. I suggest that this is because we have a messed-up relationship with pleasure in general, and food in particular, and that we need to learn how to receive God's gifts of pleasure and leisure.

IRISH DRINKERS AND AMERICAN EATERS

In the mid-twentieth century, Yale University set up a center to study alcoholism. One of their longest-term projects focused on two immigrant groups in New Haven, Connecticut: Irish and Italians. On average, people from each group drank about the same amount of alcohol. But while alcoholism and harm from drinking (disease, accidents, fighting) were nearly absent among the Italians, they were sky-high among the Irish. How could this be?

The difference, researchers concluded, was in the ways they were drinking. Italians almost entirely stuck with red

Feasting

wine and drank it at meals with family and friends (usually lunch and dinner, sometimes breakfast!). They drank plenty of it, but almost never got drunk. In a sense, wine was food for them—food that brought gladness of heart (Ps. 104:15). By contrast, the drinking of the Irish was often furtive and guilty: Irish men would stay sober all day and around their families, then head to taverns to drink whiskey and beer at night, often until they were blackout drunk. For the Irish of New Haven, moderate, family-friendly drinking was off the table: drink was a way to forget sorrow. And as anyone who is or is close to an alcoholic can testify, that way of forgetting only leads to *more* sorrow.

In her book *The Spirituality of Wine,* Gisela Kreglinger points out that total abstinence and prohibition movements tend to arise in whiskey cultures, rather than wine countries. A report on alcohol use in Ireland speaks of "the Irish tendency to view alcohol in extreme terms—that is, good versus evil; abstinent versus drunk. For this reason, the Irish are likely to deal with an alcohol problem by embracing abstinence more easily than other ethnic groups do. . . . Ireland has a higher proportion of lifetime abstainers than almost any country outside the Islamic world."

Although the United States now produces (and drinks) plenty of wine, it is historically a whiskey country and instituted nationwide prohibition by constitutional amendment for thirteen years. When it started, Prohibition was an extremely popular idea, which shows how damaging alcohol use was in the early 1900s. In my lifetime—and I am in middle age, a "young Gen-Xer"—I have seen a shift in my own and some other Christian traditions, from prohibitionism to gleeful bibbing, when it comes to alcohol and tobacco. This may be a victory for liberty of conscience, but it's not particularly a victory for holiness. Those who drink responsibly need to be humble about it. We have to remember not only what many suffer because of irresponsible drinking but also that we are never immune to temptation and sin.

I think we tend to view pleasure like the Irish view drinking: pleasure is either guilty or it's not pleasure. This is certainly true of food. Maybe we go through the McDonald's drive-thru and eat in the car because it's convenient—or maybe because we feel ashamed of liking this crazy delicious food. Chocolate advertisements describe their product as "decadent," "devilish," "sinful." I lived near a posh bakery-coffee shop called "Sin." (I felt like going in and asking *which* sin they wanted to express their support for: Coveting? Adultery? Or maybe something a little dearer to our liberal neighborhood's heart, like Racism or Domestic Violence?) It's stupid, but it's clear why someone would name a public restaurant for iniquity: we think of pleasure and guilt as going together. Pleasure is personal, private, perverted.

ABBONDANZA

Let me show you a better way.

My father used to say that he converted to Italian when he married my mother. Dad was a WASP (White Anglo-Saxon Protestant) with roots in New York and New England. Mom was half Sicilian, and half German-Canadian. Mom and Dad married young and learned to cook together. It was one of their favorite things to do. Mom was (and is) a casually, intuitively excellent cook: she just *knows* how food works, improvises, and makes remarkable meals out of all kinds of ingredients. Dad was, for years before his death, a scientific and curious baker of bread and smoker of meat. They both loved to grow their own food. They made a great team.

But Dad didn't just like cooking and eating: he loved sharing—particularly on Sundays after church. Outside one house he built, there was a big patio, the foundation of a long-gone barn. There he would set a table and many chairs in fine weather, grilling whenever he could. He would take guests behind the house to tour his vegetable garden, which was huge (one year he grew ten varieties of potato). Guests and family would sit together in the shade, Dad would give thanks, we would eat, and then the adults would chat and eat even more and the kids would read or play for the rest of the afternoon.

Dad's favorite movie was *Babette's Feast*, an absurdly slow Danish film about the reconciliation of a feuding village over an extraordinary gourmet meal, cooked by a mysterious guest (Babette). Eventually Dad found an Italian word to cover his personal idea of a good time, especially a good Sunday: *abbondanza,* abundance. Dad knew that pleasure (the enjoyment of God's gifts) and leisure (time for pleasure, particularly with others) are *good.* Ancient Israel spent a remarkable portion of the year's produce during a handful of annual festivals. In Esther and Nehemiah the Jews responded to God's mercy by feasting. In his parables Jesus always spoke of heaven as a banquet.

In their hearts, the whole world loves a feast. On holidays we buy and eat the best food (even if we've been eating too well the other days!). Few people pick a holiday as the day to start a new diet. Mom and the aunties make enough pie to feed an army on Thanksgiving. The neighborhood men trade barbecue tips and the haze of grilling fills the air on the Fourth of July.

How often should we feast? Not *all* the time: not if we want to reach old age. To feast, we have to be able to *not* feast most of the time. You have to be able to simply eat and eat simply. Missionary friends in South Sudan tell of eating the local diet: a bland sorghum paste with a sauce made of greens and maybe tomatoes. The local word for this paste (*kuïn*) is also the word for "food." This is every meal. Almost every day. If this sounds unbearable, consider that this is how most people have lived through most of time. Food is

Feasting

to keep you alive, not entertain you. Personal finance expert Dave Ramsey doesn't advise people in debt to quit eating, but to eat cheaply and not-very-interestingly: "Rice and beans, beans and rice!" *Delicious* food is a rare blessing. Blessed is the cook who makes cheap food taste good.

To feast, you also have to be able to fast. Jesus expected his disciples to fast, at least sometimes: "When you fast, anoint your head and wash your face" (Matt. 6:17). Not if, but *when*. According to one early church document, it was normal for Christians of the first century to fast twice a week on Wednesdays and Fridays. Jesus warned against advertising our fasting (or our prayer or our generosity), trying to be seen by men (rather than God, whose attention we are really seeking).

Sometimes you don't see what's missing from your life until you experience something different. I remember the time I got a full night's sleep in college. It was astounding how good I felt that day, and how interesting the lectures were! A real feast can reveal that we are always *kind of* feasting, but never really. We eat tasty food all the time. Packaged food and restaurant food are literally engineered to make our mouths water for them. But a real feast—a gathering of people, celebrating, eating and drinking the best—*that* highlights that when every meal is special, no meal is special. A real feast highlights that we don't often fast and we don't like ordinary, unexciting meals.

There is no lack of Bible verses that address gluttony. Being a glutton can either mean you eat all the time or you are such a "foodie" that you reject anything but the finest and best. (Personally, I'm tempted to do both.) "The drunkard and the glutton will come to poverty" (Prov. 23:21). Jesus was accused of being a glutton and a drunkard because he *did* feast while John the Baptist was said to have a demon because he lived on bugs and wild honey in the desert (Matt. 11:18–19). Paul says enemies of Christ that "their god is their belly" and they have "minds set on earthly things" (Phil. 3:18–19).

Ecclesiastes, also, teaches a balance of joy and restraint. "Let your garments be always white. Let not oil be lacking on your head" (Eccles. 9:8). In other words, wear party clothes and do your hair every day. And yet too much feasting is a sign of trouble: "Woe to you, O land, when . . . your princes feast in the morning!" (Eccles. 10:16). On the other hand, "Happy are you, O land, when . . . your princes feast at the proper time, for strength, and not for drunkenness" (v. 17).

My country, the United States of America, has not experienced nationwide poverty in nearly 100 years. We have not gone hungry on a large scale in more than 150 years. We have moved from "plenty" to a state of *ultra*-abundance. Our challenges are usually challenges of excess: a juggernaut of rich, sweet, tasty food coming at us every day. Yet we eat like anxious animals, consuming as much as we can as fast as we can. Eat, drink, and be merry, for tomorrow we die!

Does this describe everyone? Of course not. Many react to the Western culture of consuming, getting sick, and dying by instituting iron self-discipline. I find this fascinating, although I'm not good at putting it into practice, myself. Scientists, "n=1" self-experimenters, and overachievers argue over the best workout regimens, best time to get up, or best supplement stack in a thousand podcasts. There's a lot to like here: certainly there's a lot to be impressed by. I personally would love to have more discipline.

But there's also something wrong with this picture. Christians are to be disciplined, but our training is to focus on godliness, not in "optimizing" our exercise, breathing, nutrition, etc. (1 Tim. 4:6–8). Fasts are temporary. So are Nazirite vows (Num. 6), times of mourning (Gen. 50:10), sleep deprivation (2 Cor. 11:27; Ps. 127:1–2), and married people refraining from sex (1 Cor. 7:1–5). We can rightly do any of these things, for a time. But to do them perpetually is difficult (ask Samson) or impossible (if you don't eat, you die). Worse than the difficulty: it can be an insult to our Creator himself, who made a world of abundance, not scarcity. Paul says that it is "liars" who "forbid marriage and require abstinence from foods that God created to be received with thanksgiving by those who believe and know the truth" (1 Tim. 4:2–3). God is more glorified by the prayer at the beginning of a joyful Sunday dinner than he is by rock-hard abs or a masters team record in the Boston Marathon (as admirable as those achievements are).

The "optimizer," the man of iron discipline, sees a damaged world and says, "I can fix that." The Christian knows that only God can make things right. That doesn't mean we ignore problems while we wait for him to intervene, nor give up altogether on discipline and belly up to the trough. Instead, we are called to a pattern of eating, fasting, and feasting. "For everything created by God is good, and nothing is to be rejected if it is received with thanksgiving, for it is made holy by the word of God and prayer" (1 Tim. 4:4–5).

SALVATION CALLS FOR A FEAST

Worship and feasting go together. The holy days of the Old Testament combined sacrificial worship with feasts. Israel was to make offerings to God and then take much of the grain, wine, and animals they had raised that year—and eat them. After the work of the year, it was time to enjoy the fruit of their labor, literally. In one passage we read that Israel was to feast on a tenth of the harvest that had to last them through the year to come, in a matter of days (Deut. 14:22–26).

Isn't this a waste? If you have all that extra food, don't eat it now: save it for seed! Sell your extra wine to the neighbors: maybe you can start to get ahead in the world! Or have *some*

Feasting

fun and *some* good meals, but not so much. You'll need that food when you head back to work.

Work is good. But rest is better. Rest crowns work.

In the book of Nehemiah, returned exiles from Babylon gathered in Jerusalem to hear the law of Moses read and explained. Ezra, the scribe, led a day-long seminar with the help of some assistants. This was probably the first reading of the Law some had ever heard, and "all the people wept as they heard the words of the Law" (Neh. 8:9). They were brokenhearted over their sin. Governor Nehemiah's response is beautiful:

> "This day is holy to the Lord your God; do not mourn or weep. . . . Go your way. Eat the fat and drink sweet wine and send portions to anyone who has nothing ready, for this day is holy to our Lord. And do not be grieved, for the joy of the Lord is your strength." So the Levites calmed all the people, saying, "Be quiet, for this day is holy; do not be grieved." And all the people went their way to eat and drink and to send portions and to make great rejoicing, because they had understood the words that were declared to them. (Neh. 8:9–12)

Faith in God is not all misery over sin. We should hate our sin, and repent of it, but we don't stay sorrowful forever.

We rejoice in God's forgiveness and love and provision. Nehemiah says that the people should (1) stop mourning and weeping over their sin, (2) feast in their own homes, and (3) send the poor and the unprepared something they can feast on.

Almost the same thing happens in the book of Esther. An official named Haman engineers a day-long purge or genocide during which it is legal to kill and loot Jews throughout the Persian Empire. But when Jewish-born Queen Esther pleads with the king for help, he allows the Jews to arm and defend themselves and then, the next day, to freely strike their enemies. Because this time "had been turned for them from sorrow into gladness and from mourning into a holiday" it became a permanent two-day holiday—"days of feasting and gladness, days for sending gifts of food to one another and gifts to the poor" (Esther 9:22). It sounds a lot like Christmas.

And what about us? If ever a disaster was turned into joy, it was the resurrection of Jesus Christ on the third day after his crucifixion. The threats of our enemies, and the far greater threat of God's judgment for sin, have been eliminated. It's time to feast. Christ is Lord and King, and he shall reign forever and ever. For that reason, the early Christians gathered and celebrated not just the ceremonial meal we call Communion (bread and wine) but a full meal called an *agapē* or "love feast" (Jude 12) on the first day of the week.

Feasting

We should celebrate the Lord's Day like most people celebrate Christmas. In cultures where Christianity is strong, Sunday dinner is a feast. In an interview on mrporter.com, Ahmir Thompson (better known as Questlove), drummer of the hip hop band the Roots, says:

> I came from a family which was big on Sunday meals. My grandmother used to cook soul food and the whole process was like a religion. They would start Sunday dinner on Thursday night. They would drown a cake in rum or whisky and let it soak. On Friday she would get her vegetables ready. Saturday—she'd start slow-cooking all the meat. Now, some 30 years later, for that very meal I ate, you could charge $300 to $400 in a high-end restaurant.

The Christian Sunday dinner is an inheritance from the Jews before us. In her beautiful book *All-of-a-Kind Family*, Sydney Taylor writes of growing up in a Jewish immigrant family on the Lower East Side of Manhattan during the early 1900s.

> The Sabbath begins Friday evening at dusk and for two days Mama was busy with her preparations. On Fridays she cleaned, cooked, and baked. On

Thursdays she shopped. Sabbath meals had to be the best of the whole week so it was most important that she shop carefully.

They were just in time to see Mama saying the prayer over the candles.

The children stood around the table watching her. A lovely feeling of peace and contentment seemed to flow out from Mama to them. Mama covered her eyes with her hands, softly murmuring a prayer in Hebrew. Thus was the Sabbath ushered in. Mama set two braided loaves of white bread on the table at Papa's place. She covered them with a clean white napkin. Then from the whatnot, she took a wine bottle full of the dark sweet red wine which Papa always made himself. She also took a small wine glass and put these on the table next to the loaves.

The children lined up before Papa. He placed his hand on each child's head, asking God's blessing for his little one. When this ceremony was over, Papa left for the synagogue.

The Sabbath ennobles even the poor. Sydney Taylor lived with a large family in a crowded apartment in a seedy part of New York. But on the Sabbath her father was a king and her mother a queen. If the Jewish day of rest is celebrated with such joy and solemnity, how much more the Christian Sabbath?

THE LOGIC OF THE FEAST

Sometimes we divide the world into things that belong to God and things that don't. Church and personal devotions are God's time. Friday night at the bar is my time with my friends. Everything else is a gray area. But that's not how the Bible talks about the world. A friend called this biblical picture "graduated holiness."

In the Bible, some things are more holy than others, but all things belong to God. If people, places, or activities seem to be outside of God's kingdom, it is not because they don't belong to him: it's because they are in rebellion against his rule or they have not yet heard of it. In the Old Testament there are many examples of this. In the last nine chapters of Ezekiel, the prophet is given a vision of a restored and redeemed Israel with God's temple at its center.

Although hard to follow in the text, when we read closely we see the temple in the exact center, a holy district for the priests and Levites in a box around it, a district for the prince around that, then new allotments for the various tribes radiating outward. The picture is strange and symbolic, but lovely: God will dwell in the midst of his people. The same picture emerges in Revelation, where the New

Jerusalem is revealed, the City of God: "They will need no light of lamp or sun, for the Lord God will be their light, and they will reign forever and ever" (Rev. 22:5). God's presence at the center of the land or the city tells us that the whole place belongs to him. The transforming presence of God is promised in Zechariah too:

> And on that day there shall be inscribed on the bells of the horses, "Holy to the LORD." And the pots in the house of the LORD shall be as the bowls before the altar. And every pot in Jerusalem and Judah shall be holy to the LORD of hosts, so that all who sacrifice may come and take of them and boil the meat of the sacrifice in them. And there shall no longer be a trader in the house of the LORD of hosts on that day. (Zech. 14:20–21)

What on earth does that mean? "Holy to the LORD" was the inscription on a plate of gold that the high priest wore on his forehead when he served in the temple (Exod. 28:36–38). Zechariah's readers would have understood what this meant: if the bells of horses are inscribed "Holy to the Lord," then *everything* is holy to the Lord! All the earth belongs to the Lord: authority (Matt. 28:19); glory (Isa. 6:1–3); saving kindness (1 Tim. 4:10). But God's people are *more* holy: they are his household (1 Tim. 3:15), his kingdom of priests

(1 Peter 2:9; Exod. 19:6; Rev. 5:10). And every day is holy to the Lord. But the Sabbath is the most holy day of the week. Because it is holy, every other day is holy.

Worship is the most holy hour of the most holy day. In it we *openly* glorify God's kingdom and his grace: we say his name in prayer, praise, and preaching. The psalms are full of this language. "Let them extol him in the congregation of the people, and praise him in the assembly of the elders" (Ps. 107:32). "Oh, magnify the LORD with me, and let us exalt his name together!" (Ps. 34:3). That holy time spills over the sides into festivity and celebration through the rest of the day. In his book *Leisure: The Basis of Culture* philosopher Joseph Pieper says that worship and feast-making always go together. That's why we call days of feasting "holidays" (from "holy day").

Walter Brueggemann points out that the *Eucharist* (which means "giving thanks" in Greek) is at the very center of Christian Sabbath keeping. This is true whether or not we celebrate the Eucharist (a.k.a. Communion, a.k.a. the Lord's Supper) on a weekly basis. Worship is at the center of our Sabbath feasting, and a feast (the Lord's Supper) is at the center of our worship. The bread and wine at the heart of the Christian Sabbath and Christian worship testify to God's pardon and love. What we believe in our hearts we also experience in our bodies: Christ came to give us joy and rest.

So glorifying God with our worship flows into glorifying him with our feasting. The center of any ancient house (in Israel, Rome, or Greece) was its garden. Instead of the garden surrounding the house, the house was built to protect the private courtyard with its fountain, fruit trees, and flowers. The center of any ancient kingdom was the palace, and ancient palaces had enormous, elaborate gardens. This is where the king and his nobles feasted. The glory of a king was seen in his feasts. At the beginning of the book of Esther, we find King Ahasuerus giving "a feast lasting for seven days in the court of the garden of the king's palace" (Esther 1:5).

By contrast, Communion, the meal our King gave us, is humble and simple. It is also humble and simple compared with the elaborate sacrifices and feasts of the Old Testament. It is therefore "portable" and accessible to all kinds of people, all over the world, in a way that the ancient feasts of palace or temple were not. It is a feast we are called to celebrate everywhere. The Jews in exile were told to treat Babylon as if it were theirs to garden (Jer. 29)—to treat it like their God owned the place (because he did). We are to do the same throughout the whole world: celebrating *at least* the feast of Communion, and *when possible* the feast of the Lord's Day.

Feasting flows from worship because rest flows from worship. Of course "rest" means more than taking a break from work (which is the focus of the Westminster documents, alongside worship). It means enjoying the fruit of our labor, just as *shalom* means not just the absence of war but the enjoyment of God's blessings, every man under his own vine and fig tree (1 Kings 4:25). Rest means ceasing from labor and enjoying God's blessings along with others. Rest and feast cannot be separated.

WESTMINSTER COULD HAVE USED SOME ITALIANS

The most important statement of faith for Presbyterians is the *Westminster Confession of Faith*, written in the 1640s by a gathering of pastors and professors called the Westminster Assembly. It's one of the finest summaries of Christian doctrine ever written. But it's not perfect. This is my opinion, but it could use improvement in its statements on the Sabbath. Everything that is said is right, as far as it goes. But the document as a whole (and the Sabbath chapter in particular) came from a time of intense controversy. Looking at that background will help us understand it better.

At the time the *Confession* was written, there was war in England between people who wanted a more traditional, Roman Catholic–style church and others who wanted a more biblical, Reformed faith. (The history of the war is complicated, and it wasn't entirely about religion.) The more Reformed group held the Westminster Assembly, a yearslong gathering of pastors and scholars that drafted important statements of faith, intended to unite the churches of

England and Scotland. Given the background of war and controversy, it shouldn't surprise us that controversy found its way into the confession they wrote. The chapter on the Christian Sabbath is very black-and-white about what it means to observe the Lord's Day:

> This Sabbath is then kept holy unto the Lord, when men, after a due preparing of their hearts, and ordering of their common affairs beforehand, do not only observe an holy rest, all the day, from their own works, words, and thoughts about their worldly employments, and recreations, but also are taken up the whole time in the public and private exercises of His worship, and in the duties of necessity and mercy.

Before the Assembly, there was a huge debate on what kinds of recreation were lawful on the Lord's Day. English Sunday pastimes included archery, dancing, bear-baiting and bull-baiting (making dogs fight the bigger animals and placing bets on the winner), May games, and Morris-dancing (semi-pagan festivities to welcome springtime), all accompanied by lots of warm English ale. Pastors pointed out that these were distractions from worship—maybe idolatrous, rowdy, and encouraging other misbehavior—and not at all restful!

Feasting

In response to the arguments between Reformed pastors and Catholic nobility (who promoted these activities), King James I of England announced a royal compromise in his 1618 *Book of Sports*. Some amusements would continue (archery, ales, dancing, and May games), while others would be prohibited (bull- and bear-baiting and bowling—which makes me wonder what exactly bowling was like in the 1600s). Because it was the king's proclamation, it had to be read aloud in the churches of England, and it made no one happy, least of all the Reformed ("Puritan") pastors. Fifteen years later, his son King Charles I reissued the book to poke his Puritan critics in the eye. Thus, when it came time to write a new statement of faith, the Puritans were not in a compromising mood. The result is what we have today: a strong emphasis on what we should not do, and not much about what we should.

What a missed opportunity! The *Confession* and the *Shorter* and *Larger Catechisms* are wonderful guides to faith and life, but they are not the Bible, and the Bible gives a fuller picture of how to enjoy the Sabbath. It is about rest in a full sense, including feasting. If I had a time machine, I would send some Italians to help out the Assembly with their Sabbath chapter. Greeks, Spaniards, or Lebanese would do, but it would have to be warm-weather people, people who understood *abbondanza*. Northern Europeans may have built the modern world, but there are things they don't easily *get*, don't feel in their guts, that people from other cultures do.

(By the way, the Westminster Assembly doesn't seem to have been totally consistent in its application of the Sabbath, either. Another document they wrote, the *Directory for Public Worship*, includes the following Lord's Day instruction for households: "That the diet on that day be so ordered, as that neither servants be unnecessarily detained from the publick worship of God, nor any other person hindered from the sanctifying that day." The implication here is that the household servants should be allowed to attend church—*not* that they should have the whole day off! Apparently, it was as unthinkable for seventeenth century English to give the servants a whole day off as it would be for us to live without electricity. I take from this a suggestion that our task is not perfection but improvement. What, with the Bible's guidance and the Spirit's wisdom, can we make *better* than it is right now?)

HOW TO FEAST

The Lord's Day is the time to feast, not fast. Sunday has always been a feast day, and we should keep it that way. Even churches that celebrate Lent forbid fasting on the first day of the week. You may not make it a day of fasting and misery, any more than you may make it a day of labor and drudgery. There are plenty of other times for fasting (Luke 5:35).

Make the day and the feast the focus of the week, and prepare ahead. Take your cue from Questlove's grandmother: think a few days ahead what to eat on Sunday. A lot of people barely plan *any* of their meals; this may start to transform the way you live, in a good way.

Make the feast restful, including restful for the cook. Keep it simple enough that you can handle doing it, and it isn't the source of undue stress. The last thing you want is for Sunday dinner to become a source of anxiety for days ahead! Remember that this isn't something we *have* to do but something we *get* to do. Keep a lid on the impulse to impress your guests. Learn to use the slow cooker and the oven timer. One of my wife's strategies is to repeatedly make one of a handful of meals every Sunday. There are people who have had the same sheet pan chicken three times in a row when visiting my house. They *love* it. Those who don't usually cook can lend a hand (as long as they don't make things worse) and they can certainly help with cleanup afterward. If you need to, feast on leftovers, pancakes, or peanut butter and jelly.

But make the feast delicious. (I know I'm talking out both sides of my mouth: consider these goals rather than rules.) In Isaiah, the salvation God brings is described as "a feast of rich food, a feast of well-aged wine, of rich food full of marrow, of aged wine well refined" (Isa. 25:6). Nehemiah says to "eat the fat" (Neh. 8:10). This is the day to eat good food! That will look different from family to family and place to place. I think of the Italian import stores of Providence or North Syracuse or Pittsburgh, smelling of olives and cured meats, or the enormous smoker my friend Topper built for church barbecues. If you drink (and I am not saying that you must or should), this is a day to imbibe. My personal preference is wine, but I think anything in moderation and with thankfulness is okay. And, of course, have dessert.

Feast to the glory of God: do so in conscious honor of God. *He* put this food on your plate and this wine in your cup: not the person who prepared it, not your paycheck, not the nice people at the store, not even the farmers that grew it. "So, whether you eat or drink, or whatever you do, do all to the glory of God" (1 Cor. 10:31).

Give thanks at the beginning of the meal, and consider having family worship at the end. Receive what you've been given with thanksgiving, making it "holy by the word of God and prayer" (1 Tim. 4:4–5). Part of glorifying God is that you share what you've been given. Have plenty for everyone, and invite those outside of your family or household to eat with you, at least sometimes. In addition to feasting and enjoyment for their own sake, this can be an act of mercy and it is a *key* opportunity for discipleship.

> Wisdom . . . has slaughtered her beasts; she has mixed her wine; she has also set her table. She has

> sent out her young women to call . . . "Whoever is simple, let him turn in here! . . . Come, eat of my bread and drink the wine I have mixed. Leave your simple ways, and live, and walk in the way of insight." (Prov. 9:1–6)

Feast, because God has provided the feast. On the way up Mount Moriah, Isaac asked Abraham, "Where is the lamb for a burnt offering?" (Gen. 22:7)—and God sent the needed sacrifice. The Lamb has come, has been offered, has given us himself to eat. We feast in his honor, both at the Communion table and in our homes. We have been invited to a meal of grace that we could not earn, like both sons were in the parable of the prodigal (Luke 15).

> On this mountain the Lord of hosts will make for
> > all peoples
> > > a feast of rich food, a feast of well-aged wine,
> > > of rich food full of marrow, of aged wine well
> > > > refined.
> And he will swallow up on this mountain
> > the covering that is cast over all peoples,
> > the veil that is spread over all nations.
> > He will swallow up death forever;
> and the Lord God will wipe away tears from all
> > > faces,

> and the reproach of his people he will take away
> from all the earth,
> for the Lord has spoken. (Isa. 25:6–8)

How can we not celebrate?

8
REST

THE FOURTH COMMANDMENT, in both Exodus and Deuteronomy, focuses on *rest*. As we have already seen, this means more than not working. But it doesn't mean less. The straightforward reading of both commandments is that one day a week we are to set aside our normal labors as much as we can, in honor of God, who set an example by resting after his work of creation and gave his people rest by redeeming them.

So it's kind of ironic that this is likely the most controversial chapter in the book. Many Christians simply do not believe that they are called to a weekly day of rest. Simple commandments can turn the way we live and think about the world upside down. Clever exegesis (interpretation of

Scripture) can get us off the hook, and we are sometimes suspicious of plain readings of biblical rules. *Never* divorce? *Always* honor the government? *Never* grumble? Just bathe in the Jordan River? Hath God really said? It can't be that simple; it can't be that *uncompromising*.

It's common to "spiritualize" commandments that we are not comfortable with. But we need very good reasons to sidestep the plain meaning of one of God's laws. Maybe we should be less suspicious of what the Bible says and more suspicious of our culture and our own hearts. In what follows I want to address some of the objections to this straightforward application of the fourth commandment, and then move on to some of the real reasons (I believe) people don't rest on the Lord's Day. Next we'll wade into the wide world of first-century Pharisaism, and see how *not* to be a Pharisee as we seek to keep the Lord's Day. Finally, we'll wrap up by looking at how to rest on the Christian Sabbath.

Objection 1: The Sabbath was a law for the political nation of Israel, not the Christian Church.

According to this argument, there are certain Old Testament laws that only governed Israel, not Christians today. The *Westminster Confession* divides the law of Moses into three categories: moral, civil, and ceremonial. Moral laws are universal commandments for all time. Civil laws govern the ancient "commonwealth" of Israel, that is, the political nation. Ceremonial laws (about sacrifices, the priesthood, and so on) have passed away because they are fulfilled by the coming and crucifixion of Christ, our true priest and true sacrifice. What kind of law is the Sabbath?

A couple of clues tell us that the Sabbath (however we are to keep it) belongs to the *moral* category. First, the Sabbath dates to creation, not to the time of Moses. That puts it in the same category as marriage—something that, Jesus points out, is "from the beginning" (Matt. 19:8). And as with marriage, it's easy to lose track of the heart of the Sabbath in the details of application in the law of Moses. Also, it is rooted in the example of God himself, who did not need to rest, but rested at the end of creation to show us that we do need to rest and should rest. We imitate God because we are made in his image. The story of creation gives us a fundamental pattern, lost in the centuries of slavery in Egypt, recovered at the time of the exodus, and fulfilled and broadened in Christ.

Second, if the Sabbath commandment no longer applies, it's the only one of the Ten to simply disappear! Some object that Jesus didn't ever explicitly quote the fourth commandment. But the fact that he quotes from all the rest at one time or another indicates that the "Big Ten" are a special, authoritative list, with a continuing role in his disciples' lives. To say that because he didn't explicitly repeat one commandment means that it's gone, is the worst kind of "argument from silence"—a dangerous kind of reasoning and often a logical fallacy. But the icing on the cake is simply this: Jesus himself *kept* the Sabbath. When he was accused of breaking it, he explained that he was keeping it better than his accusers understood (Luke 6:9). If he regarded it as simply passing away, why bother?

Objection 2: We don't see the early church keeping the Lord's Day as a day of rest.

As we saw in the worship chapter, the early church *did* keep the Sabbath in the only way most of them could: by gathering for worship. On the first day of the week, churches came together for the Word and Sacrament, often meeting late into the night (possibly the only time some of them were free to meet). Early documents, including trial records of Romans accused of practicing Christianity, give a picture of people quietly passing through streets that are either empty (pre-dawn) or dangerous (after sundown) to gather for worship in homes, illegally or semi-legally. Under these circumstances, openly taking the first day of the week as a day of rest was risky. For slaves, it was impossible.

But when Christianity gained wider respect, especially in the 300s when Emperor Constantine declared it a lawful religion and made Sunday a holiday, Christians rested on the Lord's Day as well. The Council of Laodicea is evidence of that. The doctrine and practice of the Lord's Day took some centuries to take their clear form, but the same is true of the doctrine of the Trinity. Should that bother us?

The gospel changes the world, not through sudden violent revolution, but through a "patient ferment" (the title of an excellent book by Alan Kreider). We see this in many areas. Christianity did not demand the overturn of slavery in the ancient world, but by treating slaves as people and as the moral equals of their masters, it dissolved the basic beliefs that allowed slavery to make sense. Christian missions have been eroding polygamous societies for centuries, and don't usually do so by demanding an immediate divorce from wives 2, 3, 4, etc., but by forbidding additional marriages and banning men in polygamous marriages from holding church office. The Word of God critiques all of these practices without demanding sweeping changes all at once. (That said, there are practices that do demand immediate change: infanticide or idol worship, for example.)

We rest on the Lord's Day but not "at all costs." The Maccabees, a Jewish clan that led a revolt against their pagan overlords in the time between the Old and New Testaments, had to figure out their Sabbath keeping quickly. Strict interpreters of the Law, they at first attempted to carry out an insurgency without fighting on the Sabbath. It's no surprise that this was a disaster, and they concluded that it would please God if they carried out their holy war on his holy day when necessary! For similar reasons, quitting your job may be the only way to avoid Sunday work. If that means someone cannot provide for their family, I don't usually recommend it. But I often recommend changing jobs.

The ancient church was patient as they waited for the rulers and societies around them to "make room" for their faith, including their Sabbath. We too can afford to be patient. Jesus is Lord, and his kingdom will prevail. Unlike many of the ancient Pharisees, our trust is not in the perfection and thoroughness of our obedience, but in the perfection and thoroughness of *Christ's* obedience: he is our rest. Paul and the other apostles knew that pastoring is the art of the possible!

Objection 3: We can rest spiritually without resting physically.

That is spiritual indeed! I am not so spiritual that I can simply maintain my regular concerns and priorities but somehow "inwardly" be keeping the Sabbath. You cannot just add a layer of "spiritual rest" to a pile of work and worry. Rest requires *clearing time*, as well as calming our hearts.

There are times of emergency, when we have no choice: when we *cannot* rest, and the "the highways to Zion" can only be experienced in our hearts, not with our bodies (Ps. 84:5). But when we delight in something—good food, a beautiful view, a husband or wife—we do so with our bodies. And we delight in God when we use our bodies to delight in his Sabbath (Isa. 58:13–14).

Sabbath and marriage are both creation ordinances and they have similarities here as well. Marriage is not marriage without physical union. It's more than physical union, but it's not less. There are situations where something goes wrong with the physical union and natural children are impossible: in that situation the couple will have spiritual children only (through adoption, discipling, foster care, etc.). This is a hard experience: not something many people want or wish on others. In the same way, we may not have the option to rest our bodies on the Lord's Day and can only rest spiritually (in public, or at least private worship)—but this is not something we should choose, any more than a Christian couple should choose to remain childless. Most healthy marriages will yield children of both our bodies and our spirits. Likewise, Sabbath rest is more than physical rest, but it's not less.

Objection 4: I can't possibly do everything I need to in six days!

You are absolutely right. You cannot do everything that you should in six days. Or in seven. Or in a lifetime, for that matter. Wisdom begins with a recognition of the limits God has set for us: "what is man that you are mindful of him, and the son of man that you care for him?" (Ps. 8:4).

A wise man once said, the first thing to do is accept that there is more good work to do than you can ever possibly get done. The second thing to do is prioritize. Figuring out what the first things are is the most important thing to do. And for Christians, honoring God is the highest priority: we give him the "firstfruits" of all we have, including our time. If we cannot rest, cannot set aside work even at God's Word, we are still in servitude and need God to rescue us from Egypt.

REAL REASONS WE DON'T REST

There are reasons we don't rest on the Sabbath, and they're usually not the ones we give other people. Let me get a little mean.

The first reason we don't rest is that *we're rich, and the rich seldom appreciate the Sabbath like the poor do.* If you are reading this, you are probably (by world standards) quite wealthy. And the rich can choose their own times to rest: they take vacations, enjoy sabbaticals, have weekend houses, and plan for retirement. This is built into being rich, and it's great: I hope that you all have more money and leisure than you know what to do with! But this personal access to leisure has a dark side.

It is profitable for producers to keep commerce going seven days a week, and it's convenient for consumers for commerce to keep going seven days a week. Who loses out? The low-level worker.

Rest

Business will never rest unless you make it. Business is exciting, fun, competitive, and might even make you rich. Nehemiah records his aggravation with the Jewish and Gentile merchants in Jerusalem:

> In those days I saw in Judah people treading winepresses on the Sabbath, and bringing in heaps of grain and loading them on donkeys, and also wine, grapes, figs, and all kinds of loads, which they brought into Jerusalem on the Sabbath day. And I warned them on the day when they sold food. Tyrians also, who lived in the city, brought in fish and all kinds of goods and sold them on the Sabbath to the people of Judah, in Jerusalem itself! (Neh. 13:15–16)

The merchants figure they can wait Nehemiah out.

> As soon as it began to grow dark at the gates of Jerusalem before the Sabbath, I commanded that the doors should be shut and gave orders that they should not be opened until after the Sabbath. And I stationed some of my servants at the gates, that no load might be brought in on the Sabbath day. Then the merchants and sellers of all kinds of wares lodged outside Jerusalem once or twice. But I

warned them and said to them, "Why do you lodge outside the wall? If you do so again, I will lay hands on you." From that time on they did not come on the Sabbath. (vv. 19–21)

I find this passage, frankly, hilarious. The picture of fish sellers waiting, pitching tents outside Jerusalem, baskets of stinky fish and all, while a fuming Governor Nehemiah paces the city wall, is priceless. But it's a good example of the need for government to limit business at times for the sake of obedience to God. Nehemiah had read the words of the prophets from before the exile. He knew that shutting down the markets for the Sabbath was not just a matter of ceremonial purity: Sabbath breaking is a key to all kinds of oppression.

To business owners I say: you should normally shut down on the Lord's Day. There are emergencies, but by their nature, emergencies are short-term. It's better for you to risk failure in business than to disobey and distrust the Lord. Remember Daniel and his three friends, refusing to eat the king's food or bow before his golden image. Your God whom you serve is able to save you from going out of business. But it's better to obey him and go under than serve gold and dishonor him.

The second reason we don't rest is that *we feel compelled to keep working*. We *like* working. We feel a need to prove ourselves by "getting after it." We don't feel as good standing still. But working constantly is slavery, and that's true if someone is behind you with a whip forcing you *or* if you are addicted to your work, wired to drive, compete, go go go!

Freedom doesn't simply consist in "doing whatever you want," because sin twists and damages our desires. Every human heart, even the heart of a Christian, is a warzone. "For the desires of the flesh are against the Spirit, and the desires of the Spirit are against the flesh, for these are opposed to each other, to keep you from doing the things you want to do" (Gal. 5:17). Freedom is joyfully living to the highest capacity of our created nature. In heaven, that means the experience of God's presence. In this world it means working and resting. Constant work is slavery, whether we like it and choose it, or whether we hate it. If you're stuck, you're stuck. Pray to get unstuck. Paul's counsel is helpful in either case. "Were you a bondservant when called? Do not be concerned about it. (But if you can gain your freedom, avail yourself of the opportunity)" (1 Cor. 7:21). You can serve Christ as a slave. But if you can get free, that's better.

Our world is closer to the world of Egypt than we think. It is a world of "total work" (to use Josef Pieper's phrase), a system where we live to work and are defined by our work. But total work is a false gospel (a heresy), and a life of constant work is practicing a false discipleship (a "heteropraxy"). One ancient heretic, Pelagius, taught that there is no such thing as original sin: we could all overcome our shortcomings and achieve salvation if we chose to put in the work. There are a lot of Pelagians in the world. Some "put in the work" by putting in the work: constantly driving and striving in their career, field, institution, or sport. Some "put in the work" (ironically) by displaying their religious behavior, even making a show of their Sabbath keeping (we'll explore this in a moment).

Any message of self-salvation is a crushing false gospel. Life and death, success and failure, are in the hand of God. Everything we have is a gift, and every gift is an opportunity to glorify and enjoy God. He gives us work to do, not because he needs our help to provide for our needs or better the world, but so that we may know him better by imitating him. And he gives us rest in order to know him *even better* as we imitate his rest and enjoyment: enjoyment of what we have done, but especially of what he has done.

There are other reasons we don't rest. Maybe *we think we need more money*. Well, sometimes we do. Poverty is not fun, and it's a lot harder to get out of than some people think. If you are poor and a Christian, this is not a private issue; not something to face alone. Get your church praying, seeking, thinking, advising, and helping. If at all possible, make a plan for your betterment. But keep in mind that there's a blurry line between needing more and wanting more. "Consider the lilies," Jesus says. If God will clothe grass so beautifully, won't he take care of you? "But seek first the kingdom of God and his righteousness, and all these things will be added to you" (Matt. 6:28, 33). "The love of money is a root of all kinds of evils. It is through craving that some have wandered away from the faith and pierced themselves with many pangs" (1 Tim. 6:10). "Keep your life free from love of money, and be content with what you have, for he has said, 'I will never leave you nor forsake you'" (Heb. 13:5). Don't steal from the Lord what belongs to him, whether time or money (Eph. 4:28). Honor him with the first of your wealth and the first day of your week (Prov. 3:9).

Maybe *we haven't learned to plan our time*. This is a huge issue for students in high school or college, but also for adults of all ages. If this is your situation, I can tell you that there is enormous freedom in knowing that you *may not* catch up on homework on Sunday. As far as school goes, Sunday doesn't exist. Keeping the Lord's Day may be the first step in learning to plan your time (it was for me). You are capable of more than you know. Don't wait until you "learn time management" to start keeping the Lord's Day: keep the day holy, and let that reshape your week.

Maybe (and this is an ugly secret for some) *we feel more at home in our workplace than at home or church*. Either the work itself is absorbing and enjoyable, or we experience appreciation, respect, and status at work more than elsewhere. If this is you, there's a lot more to figure out than

Sabbath keeping. Status in the world does not translate to status in the kingdom of God, where "many who are first will be last, and the last first" (Mark 10:31). The King of kings was among us "as one who serves" (Luke 22:27). In the ancient church, slaves sometimes held office and authority over their own masters. If you want to enter the kingdom, you must become like a little child. That means humility, accepting that you are a student of Christ and not a pro.

You may need to adjust your priorities and pursue those of the kingdom: humility, love, and service. If you have a family, that is your first field of service: not work, not even church. I have seen some Christians, especially pastors and elders, sacrifice family for church. That is not the way of Christ, either.

THE PHARISEE SABBATH

Jesus spoke some of his harshest words to "scribes and Pharisees, hypocrites!" (in Matthew 23—and many other places). One of the most frequent battles they fought was over Sabbath keeping: the Pharisees were strict and did not think Jesus was strict enough.

Now, it's easy to pick on the Pharisees. Religious authorities—especially those of a different religion—are low-hanging fruit for ridicule. But Jesus's criticism was not cheap. One reason he probably gave them so much grief is that of all the "parties" of ancient Judaism, they were the closest to him in doctrine. Like Jesus, they had a strong sense of the authority of God in salvation. Like Jesus, they taught against the revolutionary activities of their day (most of the time). And on key issues like the coming resurrection and the existence of angels, they were on the same side as Jesus against the Sadducees, who did not believe in those things (Matt. 22:30; Acts 23:8). When we see this it makes more sense that many early disciples actually came from the ranks of the Pharisees (Acts 15:5). You can't say that about the Sadducees.

Having strict rules for the Sabbath was not quite what the Pharisees got wrong. Jesus seldom attacks their rules and traditions directly. Instead, he criticizes them for *not going deep enough.* "Woe to you, scribes and Pharisees, hypocrites! For you tithe mint and dill and cumin, and have neglected the weightier matters of the law: justice and mercy and faithfulness. These you ought to have done, without neglecting the others" (Matt. 23:23). He tells his disciples that "unless your righteousness exceeds that of the scribes and Pharisees, you will never enter the kingdom of heaven" (Matt. 5:20). Clearly, Jesus did not look at the Law, or even the Pharisaic traditions, and shrug them off. "Relax!"

But the Pharisees got some things deadly wrong, including their practice of keeping the Sabbath. The details of their rules reveal what they got wrong. Their first problem was that *they failed to see that the Sabbath was given to serve the good of human beings*. For this reason they condemned Jesus for healing people on the Sabbath. His response is crucially important: "The Sabbath was made for man, not man for the Sabbath" (Mark 2:27). The Sabbath serves human good. Don't get that backward. When we reflect on the origins of the Sabbath in the creation week, and the renewal of the Sabbath for a people recently freed from slavery, we see how true this is. The Sabbath is given to bless and heal human beings.

The Pharisees should have known better. One ancient Jewish commentary on Exodus included this line: "The Sabbath is given over to you, not you to the Sabbath." But they did not stick with this principle. Instead, they created elaborate rules for what kinds of work were and weren't permitted on the Sabbath, what counted as picking up a burden and what didn't, how far one could walk on the Sabbath, and so on.

They came up with very specific answers to these questions. The resulting rules were strict, odd, and sometimes feel random. A "Sabbath day's journey" (Acts 1:12) is 2,000 cubits (about two-thirds of a mile). Walk farther and you were breaking the Sabbath. In our day, Orthodox Jews stretch a string around a large area to make it a "dwelling" within which you can carry burdens (Jer. 17:22). Each week New York City's rabbis make sure that eighteen miles of fishing line are in place around Manhattan. You can't kindle a fire on the Sabbath, but you can ask your Gentile neighbor to turn the stove on for you!

Jesus cut through the pile of rules and rulings to show the mercy of God toward the sick, the miserable, and the outsider. He described his own coming as "the year of the Lord's favor" (Luke 4:19), like the ancient Sabbath and Jubilee years. The Pharisees had separated "rest" from "mercy" (the Sabbath day from its meaning). They had turned the Sabbath into a religious performance, a mark of purity, rather than a joyful act of faith in God who provides: *Jehovah-jireh*, as he is called in Genesis 22:14.

Jesus healed a woman who walked bent for nearly two decades, and he got flak for it from the synagogue ruler. He responded:

> Does not each of you on the Sabbath untie his ox or his donkey from the manger and lead it away to water it? And ought not this woman, a daughter of Abraham whom Satan bound for eighteen years, be loosed from this bond on the Sabbath day? (Luke 13:15–16)

But the Pharisees had a problem bigger than misunderstanding the Sabbath: in their observance of the Law *they failed to pursue God's approval and instead pursued man's approval.* We generally call this what Jesus called it: *hypocrisy*.

As John put it, "they loved the glory that comes from man more than the glory that comes from God" (John 12:43).

We often think of hypocrisy as "saying one thing and doing another." But it's more subtle than that. Sometimes people behave inconsistently simply because they're sinners and they sin. A hypocrite, however, behaves one way when he thinks other people see him and another when they aren't looking. He is a practical atheist, no matter what faith he professes. By contrast Jesus taught his disciples to obey for one audience, God:

> Beware of practicing your righteousness before other people in order to be seen by them, for then you will have no reward from your Father who is in heaven. Thus, when you give to the needy, sound no trumpet before you, as the hypocrites do in the synagogues and in the streets, that they may be praised by others. Truly, I say to you, they have received their reward. But when you give to the needy, do not let your left hand know what your right hand is doing, so that your giving may be in secret. And your Father who sees in secret will reward you. (Matt. 6:1–4)

Hypocrisy poisoned everything the Pharisees did, not just keeping the Sabbath. As seen in this chapter from

Matthew, they gave to the poor to be seen by other people. They also prayed and fasted to be noticed and praised by their neighbors. Jesus spoke against all of these things in the Sermon on the Mount.

Why did they do this? The Pharisees figured out that religious performance (the word "hypocrite" comes from the Greek for "actor") is amazingly powerful. Unlike the Sadducees, the priestly clans, the desert colonists, or the Herodians (rich collaborators with the Romans), the Pharisees were very much "of the people." Many came from the same farming, fishing, or trade background that Jesus and most of his disciples did. When they spoke, they had the ear of the "people of the land" (the *am ha-aretz* in Hebrew). Religious performance was, and is, a way to be upwardly mobile: they signaled their virtue in order to impress regular folks and get ahead.

Now, there were many good and godly people among the Pharisees, and especially the trained scribes. Their way of looking at the Hebrew Bible had value. But as a group, they turned their biblical expertise into a tool for gaining respect. Respect became business opportunities, and business opportunities became oppression.

> Beware of the scribes, who like to walk around in long robes and like greetings in the marketplaces and have the best seats in the synagogues and

the places of honor at feasts, who devour widows' houses and for a pretense make long prayers. They will receive the greater condemnation. (Mark 12:38–40)

In this way, the life-giving commandments of God became weapons, tools to exploit the poor, the illiterate, and the inarticulate. No wonder the Master—and at later points, his apostles—tore them apart.

HOW NOT TO BE A PHARISEE

We had better pay attention to the cannon fire Jesus directed at the scribes and Pharisees because any community that takes its principles seriously, and tries to live them out consistently and conscientiously, runs the risk of hypocrisy. Serious Christians are in danger of the same sins. But we must take obedience seriously. In fact, we need to take it *more* seriously than the Pharisees did. So how do we keep the Lord's Day? How do we obey God's rules but not be Pharisees about it?

Beware of the perfect system. The Law may be simple, but that doesn't mean obeying it will be simple or easy. If you come up with a comprehensive list of rules that will "idiot-proof" any command, your list is either not practical or not complete (or both). This was part of Jesus's point when he talked about various commandments this way:

> You have heard that it was said to those of old, "You shall not murder; and whoever murders will be liable to judgment." But I say to you that everyone who is angry with his brother will be liable to judgment; whoever insults his brother will be liable to the council; and whoever says, "You fool!" will be liable to the hell of fire. (Matt. 5:21–22)

In the case of the Sabbath, the demands of mercy sometimes override the commandment to rest: so Jesus taught. To put it another way, mercy rules and even defines rest. No human interpretation of the Bible can plan for everything ahead of time. Keep your Bible and your mind open.

Focus on giving rest to others. The Pharisees took rest for themselves but failed to give rest to others, especially those in the most need of mercy and help. As a result even their own Sabbaths weren't real rest but a "performance" of rest. This is not ultimately a matter of either/or. We must do both. We delight in the Sabbath (Isa. 58:13) when we both enjoy it *and* share it with others.

Learn to keep it before you start telling others to. This is not an absolute rule and neither were Jesus's statements about giving to the poor, fasting, and praying in secret. I know that this is funny advice from someone writing a book on keeping the Lord's Day, but it is not necessary to tell everyone about your Sabbath habits. We have to balance our responsibility to teach and disciple others (starting with our own families) with the terrible temptation of making the Sabbath a performance. James gives wise counsel: "Who is wise and understanding among you? By his good conduct let him show his works in the meekness of wisdom" (James 3:13). Wisdom is a matter of doing, not talking. Learn to do before you talk.

And don't ever boast in your Sabbath keeping:

Thus says the Lord:
"Let not the wise man boast in his wisdom, let not the mighty man boast in his might, let not the rich man boast in his riches, but let him who boasts boast in this, that he understands and knows me, that I am the LORD who practices steadfast love, justice, and righteousness in the earth. For in these things I delight, declares the LORD." (Jer. 9:23–24)

It is the Lord and his grace, not your service to him, that let you stand up straight and look the world in the eye.

The flipside of this principle is: *be slow to judge others for their Sabbath keeping.* "Judge not!" gets over-quoted, but it is the word of Christ. What did he mean? The full saying is this: "Judge not, that you be not judged. For with the judgment you pronounce you will be judged, and with the measure you use it will be measured to you" (Matt. 7:1). Elsewhere

Jesus actually tells his disciples *to judge*—but to do so with caution and fairness: "Do not judge by appearances, but judge with right judgment" (John 7:24). We could sum these up to say, judge only if and when it is necessary, and bend over backward to avoid prejudice and unfairness. There is no glory in suffering for being a meddler (1 Peter 4:15). In the freedom of the gospel, every person's and every household's obedience is going to look slightly different, because every person and situation are somewhat unique.

Always keep in mind that the Sabbath is for man, not man for the Sabbath. Like all principles of grace, this can be twisted into an excuse for lawlessness. But the abuse of something doesn't take away its use. The works of Jesus in relieving misery and displaying the compassion of the kingdom of God teach us: no one should truly suffer in the name of Sabbath rest. The day is intended to give life and joy, like water to desert lands.

THE CHRISTIAN SABBATH

When Israel ate manna in the wilderness, God gave them enough for two days on the day before the Sabbath, then didn't send any on the Sabbath. The sending of the manna, but even more the double-provision on the sixth day, taught them that God is their provider: "I am the LORD your God, who brought you up out of the land of Egypt. Open your mouth wide, and I will fill it" (Ps. 81:10).

The Lord's Day, always pointing us to the resurrection of Jesus, teaches us that salvation, which we could never earn, belongs to our Lord (Ps. 3:8; Jon. 2:9; Rev. 7:10; 19:1). Rest is even more fitting for celebrating the New Covenant than it was for the Old Covenant. Although salvation in the Old was gracious, a free gift, that wasn't clear to many: law, not grace, was in the foreground. That was the weakness of the Law, and it led many Jews to live "as if it were based on works" (Rom. 9:32).

In the New Covenant it is overwhelmingly clear that salvation comes from the work of another—Jesus Christ the Lord. We are offered grace that can't be bought with anything we could offer. And so the promises of the Old Covenant are fulfilled in the New:

> Come, everyone who thirsts, come to the waters; and he who has no money, come, buy and eat! Come, buy wine and milk without money and without price. Why do you spend your money for that which is not bread, and your labor for that which does not satisfy? Listen diligently to me, and eat what is good, and delight yourselves in rich food. (Isa. 55:1–2)

Jesus is the keeper of these promises: "all the promises of God find their Yes in him" (2 Cor. 1:20). At the dawn of his public ministry, he read aloud in a synagogue the following words of Isaiah: "The Spirit of the Lord is upon me, because he has anointed me to proclaim good news to the poor. He has sent me to proclaim liberty to the captives and recovering of sight to the blind, to set at liberty those who are oppressed, to proclaim the year of the Lord's favor" (Luke 4:18–19; cf. Isa. 61:1–2). Then he sat down on the teacher's seat and announced: "Today this Scripture has been fulfilled in your hearing" (Luke 4:21).

Jesus described himself as "Lord of the Sabbath" (Matt. 12:8; Luke 6:5). I used to read this as Jesus claiming authority over the Sabbath: "I made it, I rule over it, I define it, I will say what is and isn't keeping it." Now I think he means more. The claim that he is Lord of the Sabbath is connected to his announcement of the year of the Lord's favor. He is the walking, talking, dying, rising Sabbath. He is the embodiment of Sabbath and Jubilee, and without him there can be no rest, forgiveness, or freedom.

Life is hard. So hard that God alone can help us. It is better to pray than to worry and work. Anxiety grips us, largely because we *still* think, no matter how many sermons on grace we've heard, that if we try hard enough, we can save ourselves from disaster and ensure a good life. Every great civilization thinks so. Like Babel, we have done astonishing things, seemingly through the power of work and striving. Our world shouts at us constantly that if we don't work harder, all will be lost.

But Jesus undermines our confidence in the power of work, anxiety, and trying harder:

> And which of you by being anxious can add a single hour to his span of life? If then you are not able to do as small a thing as that, why are you anxious about the rest? Consider the lilies, how they grow: they neither toil nor spin, yet I tell you, even Solomon in all his glory was not arrayed like one of these. But if God so clothes the grass, which is alive in the field today, and tomorrow is thrown into the oven, how much more will he clothe you, O you of little faith! And do not seek what you are to eat and what you are to drink, nor be worried. For all the nations of the world seek after these things, and your Father knows that you need them. Instead, seek his kingdom, and these things will be added to you. (Luke 12:25–31)

Elsewhere Paul contrasts anxiety and prayer:

> Rejoice in the Lord always; again I will say, rejoice. Let your reasonableness be known to everyone. The Lord is at hand; do not be anxious about anything, but in everything by prayer and supplication with thanksgiving let your requests be made known to

God. And the peace of God, which surpasses all understanding, will guard your hearts and your minds in Christ Jesus. (Phil. 4:4–7)

So how will we live? What will we eat? While the New Testament occasionally instructs lazy believers to work (Eph. 4:28; 2 Thess. 3:10), it calls us more urgently to a life of prayer: asking Another to give us what we need as a free gift. The first petition in the Lord's Prayer is the petition of beggars: "give us this day our daily bread" (Matt. 6:11). What does it mean to seek first the kingdom of God? Sometimes it means working, when doing so honors him and loves our neighbors. Sometimes it means resting. Always it means prayer.

God rested on the seventh day after finishing his work of creation. As Jesus finished his work of redemption, he cried out, "It is finished!" (John 19:30). On the Lord's Day, Christians rest in honor of Christ's finished work. When he rose he established a new and joyful Sabbath. We rest and reflect on the good that God has done in creation, but *even more* what he has done in the death and resurrection of Jesus Christ.

HOW TO REST ON THE LORD'S DAY

The Westminster documents are even more serious about the Sabbath than most Reformed confessions. One question of the *Larger Catechism* asks, "How is the sabbath or the Lord's day to be sanctified?"

> A. The sabbath or Lord's day is to be sanctified by an holy resting all the day, not only from such works as are at all times sinful, but even from such worldly employments and recreations as are on other days lawful; and making it our delight to spend the whole time (except so much of it as is to be taken up in works of necessity and mercy) in the public and private exercises of God's worship: and, to that end, we are to prepare our hearts, and with such foresight, diligence, and moderation, to dispose, and seasonably to despatch our worldly business, that we may be the more free and fit for the duties of that day.

Simply put, we are called to rest entirely from our regular work and spend the day in worship, and we need to prepare to do both. Westminster doesn't actually spell out the details the way the Jews did; we are to keep focused on Christ and the "weightier matters of the law" (Matt. 23:23). But what should this rest look like? As before (and keeping in mind the danger of being a Pharisee!) I want to give counsel, a mix of principles, and specific suggestions.

Take the Lord's Day seriously: *stop working and rest on the first day of the week*. Trust God to meet your needs, be content with a little less than you could be doing or earning, cut back your lifestyle if necessary, and get your work and shopping done by Saturday night. You're not going to do this perfectly: there is no checklist for a flawless Sabbath. Be patient with yourself and be slow to judge others. When you fail, don't give up: try again next week.

Encourage the anxious and conscientious to rest—family, fellow Christians, even unbelievers. Maybe you're not the anxious one: your wife or husband or parents or children are. With patience call them to lay their burdens and concerns at the feet of God and honor him with the day. When you see non-Christian friends struggling with exhaustion and burnout, you have an opportunity to share your practice. Better than that, you have an opportunity to explain *why* you rest on the Lord's Day. And the answer cannot be merely "God says to." You heard Christ's invitation to those who labor and are heavy laden (Matt. 11:28): pass it on.

Rest your mind as well as your body. Many people today are "knowledge workers" rather than people who labor with their hands and their backs. That might mean that (non-competitive) sports or gentle exercise are genuinely restful. My father often went for a long walk with his kids after a Sunday nap, in the woods or in a riverside park, and smoked a cigar.

Opt out of the contemporary communications ecosystem. In other words, *ignore your phone, turn off the computers and TV, and let these tools rest.* This is mainly a way for *you* to rest: I don't know if God has the same concern for iPhones that he does for oxen and asses: probably not. There is an enormous need for deep thinking on the role of technology in our lives: I don't think a deep and well-developed theology of technology has formed, and our confession and catechisms are 450 years old. But the Sabbath gives us a place to get out of the undertow. It is best, as Abraham Heschel said, "to have them and to be able to do without them."

Prepare for the day: *get laundry, shopping, work, etc., done ahead and get enough sleep.* Our deadline is Saturday night, not Monday morning. Sunday should be the beginning of a new week, not catch-up from the old. I avoid watching anything stressful or provocative on Saturday night: I don't want my mind to be full of some movie when I'm at church (and that rule predates my becoming a pastor). Work hard and honestly when you do work. Show your employers, family, and neighbors that the Sabbath is not a cloak for laziness.

There are people who have particular challenges to resting on the Lord's Day. I have in mind, first, people in high-intensity businesses, where there is an expectation of night and weekend work and 24/7 reachability. Interestingly, many in the startup world are recognizing the importance of rest. If this is your world, I suggest Jewish entrepreneur

Aaron Edelheit's book, *The Hard Break: The Case for a 24/6 Lifestyle,* as a good start. If you cannot get some margin for rest, including the Lord's Day, you may be a kind of slave, no matter how well paid you are or how promising your stock options look. Consider another line of work: wealth and business fame are not reason enough to live this way.

Another type of person with a particular challenge is the low-skilled laborer. I have in mind particularly immigrant friends with limited English who have had to start at the absolute bottom of the employment market, but they're not the only ones in this boat. Laborers can be helped with letters from their churches asking for their religious beliefs to be respected. When you can get your freedom, do. The US government expects employers to make "reasonable accommodations" for religious people's holy days, including simple things like letting them take a shift on a different day. See the letters in Appendix 2 for a helpful start.

The third group is people in medicine and other "helping professions." If this is you, your days are often spent in Christ-like mercy to the sick and suffering, and I commend you. Also, Christ did non-emergency healing on the Sabbath (even the Pharisees would have been okay with calling an ambulance for arterial bleeding). But respect your own limits. You are not Christ: you do this for a living. And you are not God: you need to rest. See if someone else can take your Sunday shift, at least some of the time, so that you can worship, rest, feast, and show other kinds of mercy.

TRY IT

If keeping the Lord's Day is new or strange to you, I encourage you to obey the Lord, then watch what he does. We are creatures of habit: our own habits, and the habits of our families and cultures. Western culture has a habit of never resting, always going. For some people, it is *terrifying* to contemplate blocking out a whole day each week for rest, hospitality, and worship. So try it, and see what happens over time.

Read what God says to those who keep his Sabbaths in Isaiah 58. Remember the double portion of manna that appeared on the sixth day of each week to feed Israel through the Sabbath. Go watch *Chariots of Fire* and meditate on the promise one competitor quotes to the Sabbath-keeping Olympic runner Eric Liddell: "Them that honour me I will honour" (1 Sam. 2:30 KJV). Pray for God's help, and see what happens to your anxiety and your family life.

I have one last word on this, and it is addressed to parents with minor children. It is *your* job to make sure your kids rest. And like many important ways you care for them, they won't necessarily appreciate it. You may have dreams of a hockey scholarship or an NFL career for them. Those dreams may be good. Or they may crush your beloved children. Start dreaming God's dreams for them instead,

- that they would flourish in God's courts when they are old (Ps. 92:13–14, "A Psalm. A Song for the Sabbath"!);
- that they (and you) would see their children's children, and peace for Israel (Ps. 128:6);
- that they will make you and God glad by their wisdom and kindness (Prov. 27:11);
- that they would rebuild ruins and restore streets: be people whose works last for generations (Isa. 58:12); and
- that they would delight themselves in the Lord (Isa. 58:13–14).

If you have a family, a circle of friends, or a church, you can lead by your patient example. Whether you are leading from the front, the back, or the middle, lead with patience and mercy. Rest on the Lord's Day, and share that rest with others.

9
MERCY

WHEN JESUS DECLARED himself "Lord of the Sabbath," he was making an enormous claim. It wasn't just that he had authority over the Sabbath (though he did and does), and it wasn't just that his ministry was in harmony with the Old Testament and its laws (though it was and is). It was that the Sabbath was *about him* all along: he brought the true rest that the Sabbath day depicted, as it still does today. The Old Covenant was one of hope; the New Covenant would be one of joy, because hope had not disappointed. Unlike Moses, his great gift was not laws that were impossible to keep, not even the command to rest, but rest itself. Rest from sin, rest from God's sentence of death for sin, rest from our endless striving—striving

Worship, Feasting, Rest, Mercy

for survival, striving for happiness, striving for recognition, even striving to "be ourselves." Our good is no longer in our hands, no longer something we must achieve. "You are not your own, for you were bought with a price" (1 Cor. 6:19–20).

Of the Ten Commandments, only the fourth and fifth ("Honor your father and mother") are phrased positively. Every other commandment starts with "Thou shalt not." But we are to *remember* the Sabbath and to do so by resting *and giving rest to others.* All ten lead us toward love for God and neighbor: the Sabbath commandment gets us to love of neighbor faster than any other.

The *Westminster Shorter Catechism* gives a pithy answer to the question, "How is the Sabbath to be sanctified [kept holy]?"

> A. The sabbath is to be sanctified by a holy resting all that day, even from such worldly employments and recreations as are lawful on other days; and spending the whole time in the public and private exercises of God's worship, except so much as is to be taken up in the works of necessity and mercy.

Westminster recognized that the teaching of Jesus tempered and reshaped the Jewish understanding of the Sabbath. With his words and his acts of healing, Jesus reconnected the

Sabbath to its fundamental theme: life-giving, health-giving, kind, merciful, joyful *rest*. This is what it meant all along. How much more, now that the Lord of the Sabbath has come in the flesh?

In this chapter, we'll look at another fundamental part of keeping the Christian Sabbath: showing mercy to those in need. First we'll look at the church's generosity as God's answer to the ticking bomb of inequality in the world. Then, we'll look at the particular meaning of the Sabbath for employers and others in positions of wealth and influence—as well as for "the rest of us." We will talk about hospitality, the "Part II" of feasting. Finally, we will look at some general principles of biblical mercy, to keep in mind in Sabbath mercy and beyond.

JESUS AND OUR MONEY

In his days on earth, Jesus was not usually around rich people. While he had some very well-known conversations with rich individuals and was ultimately accused and put to death by the wealthy and powerful ruling elites, he was raised among, recruited his disciples from, and lived and taught among regular people—often very poor people. With this in mind, it should surprise us that Jesus spoke about money as often as he did. While he was no anti-business, anti-capitalist campaigner, he often spoke of money in parables, and sometimes gave stern warnings against the love and service of money: "No one can serve two masters, for either he will hate the one and love the other, or he will be devoted to the one and despise the other. You cannot serve God and money" (Matt. 6:24). The King James Version of the Bible translates the last sentence more literally (and better): "Ye cannot serve God and mammon." The gospel, written in Greek, uses the Aramaic word for "the god of money" or maybe "Mr. Money," *mammon*. Jesus is not just talking about money, he's talking about *Money*, the Bottom Line, the god that so much of our world worships.

Jesus talked about money so much because it is powerful, whether you have it or not, and the temptation to seek and serve it is universal. How people got rich was not Jesus's only concern: he also addressed the pride, security, and self-satisfaction that having money often brings.

> "The land of a rich man produced plentifully, and he thought to himself, 'What shall I do, for I have nowhere to store my crops?' And he said, 'I will do this: I will tear down my barns and build larger ones, and there I will store all my grain and my goods. And I will say to my soul, "Soul, you have ample goods laid up for many years; relax, eat, drink, be merry."' But God said to him, 'Fool! This night your soul is required of you, and the things you have prepared, whose will they be?' So is the one who lays

up treasure for himself and is not rich toward God."
(Luke 12:16–21)

Jesus taught that the two great commandments, love of God and love of neighbor, summarize and interpret the whole law. In this parable the rich man's world has become so full of himself and his possessions that there is no room for either God or his neighbor. They are not part of his accounting process.

What does it mean to be "rich toward God"? Mostly, it means loving our neighbors who are in need: "Truly, I say to you, as you did it to one of the least of these my brothers, you did it to me" (Matt. 25:40). Even unbelievers and pagans know that we owe *something* to mankind beyond our own households. The Greeks called men who only cared about themselves and their families "private men," *idiōtai,* idiots.

God and neighbor must be part of our budgets. If we have received much, it is not so that we can hoard it or spend it on ourselves: "Everyone to whom much was given, of him much will be required, and from him to whom they entrusted much, they will demand the more" (Luke 12:48). We are given gifts like power and wealth so that we can bless others with them. The Sabbath commandment makes this clear. Most of the words in the commandment are actually about giving Sabbath rest to those under your authority: yes, you are to rest, but you are also to arrange things so that your son, daughter, servants, draft animals and other livestock, and even the non-citizen you hired rest as well (Deut. 5:14).

Keeping the Sabbath is more than a personal and private habit. It is a way of sharing the generosity and kindness of God with others, starting with those closest to us (usually our families). From there, God's rest spreads outward to the wider community. The Sabbath and Jubilee years, with slaves being freed, debts being canceled, and land returning to original grantees, were supposed to hit "reset" for Israel on a large scale. Each week we do the same on a small scale in our little corners of the world.

DEFUSING THE BOMB

I'm going to open up a can of worms, but it needs to be opened. Inequality is one of the wretched and unending problems of life in a sinful world. In the Old Testament, keeping the Sabbath was linked to care of the poor, worshiping the one true God, personal morality, and avoiding God's just judgment. Breaking the Sabbath was condemned in the same breath as oppression and sexual sin.

The Sabbath actually points us to the fundamental equality of human beings before God. It reminds the powerless and powerful alike that we are alike in the hands of God and recipients of his grace. And in a world that is staring down the barrel of God's judgment, the merciful life of the church, visible above all on the Sabbath, gives us something we can do to make things right.

Simply put, inequality means that some people wind up with larger and larger shares of the pie, while others have smaller and smaller shares. This is more or less inevitable, over time, when trade happens (and there is no real alternative to free trade). It's not absolute poverty that makes people resentful and violent, but the feeling that there are others who have vastly more than they do and they can do nothing to fix it (in the world, no matter how equally we are created, wealth means power). You can see this watching kids play the board game Monopoly: there's a point when everyone realizes that a winner is emerging, and there's pretty much no turning back. One by one other players hit what Nassim Taleb calls the ruin point: they cry "Uncle!" because they can't take it anymore. They are effectively out of the game. If the game goes on for long, tempers are lost and (depending on the age of the players) tears start to fall. The end of the game is a mercy.

But what if you can't quit the game, and the game won't end? That's essentially the problem of inequality in society. There are, as far as I can tell, three ways of thinking about it. Those on one side say, "Well, the wealthy earned what they have and they have a right to it. The people at the bottom should have made better choices. Even now, they can probably turn things around." This is the logic of Job's friends, who were certain that his misfortunes must be God's punishment for his own sins. There is definitely truth in this. Often, the wealthy *have* played by the rules. Often, the down-and-out *have* made things worse for themselves. And often, there *is* a possibility of changing direction: I have seen it happen. The path forward might be different behavior and a new attitude, pure and simple. As far as it goes, the argument is sound.

However, it does not account for the brutality of life at the bottom. There are people who face a mountain of obstacles to improving themselves or even to seeing the possibility of a better life. It also doesn't face the reality of God's varied providence. Hindus teach that if you are doing well in this life it's because you deserve to (because of your actions in a previous life). This is *karma*. As Christians, we believe that if you're doing well it's because God has poured out his kindness on you.

You may have cooperated often and made good decisions, but we are blessed by the *grace* of God, not as an act of justice on his part. And perhaps the most frightening problem with deciding we are okay with inequality is that whether or not the winners won fairly, rising inequality inevitably leads to violence: the violence of revolution, the violence of maintaining law and order, or both. Historian Walter Scheidel concludes that the only things that reliably reduce inequality are large-scale war, plague, government collapse, and revolution. Ouch.

The second approach is possibly even worse. "Inequality must be overcome *at all costs*. Therefore it is right and just to take the assets of those who have more and give them to those who have less." This is what Rudyard Kipling called "robbing selected Peter to pay collective Paul." There is a "soft" way of doing this that we generally call socialism or maybe public-private partnership. But efforts to fix inequality from the top tend to cause even more problems, because trying to run "society" or "the economy" never really works. Someone said that we used to suffer from problems, but now we suffer from solutions. There is also "hard" redistribution, Marxist communism being the clearest example. In Russia, China, and a host of other nations, redistribution led not only to violence that dwarfed the Holocaust, but also to mass imprisonment and mass starvation, as the lands of productive farmers were confiscated and made into "collectives." All this was done in the name of equality.

But there is another way—the way of Christ and his church. Jesus called his hearers, whether rich or poor, not to love or dedicate themselves to money (Matt. 6:24). Rich or poor, as they were able, they were to feed the hungry, clothe the naked, care for the sick, visit the prisoner (Matt. 25:34–40). They were to give generously (Mark 12:41–44) and quietly (Matt. 6:3), as an act of love toward God and neighbor, not as a way of impressing others.

They were to be salt and light in the world (Matt. 5:13–16), both revealing what is in darkness and preserving what is good from decay. Alongside these instructions came warnings that God's judgment was coming on Judea (Matt. 24) and Galilee (Luke 13:1–2). Is this a coincidence?

Jesus taught his followers to practice generosity and kindness—*voluntary* redistribution—that could reverse the decay of society and might even turn away the wrath of God, as he relented from destroying Nineveh (see Jon. 4:11; Matt. 12:41). The Jerusalem church in the early chapters of Acts lived this out consciously and seriously. God's judgment on Jerusalem was near at hand (Acts 2:19–21, 36, 40). With "the end of the world as we know it" on the horizon, many of the church's wealthy were happy to sell off properties and use the proceeds to feed the hungry within (and possibly beyond) the church (Acts 2:42–47; 4:32–37; 6:1–7). This was living the life of heaven on earth, and preventing (or delaying) their corner of earth from descending into hell. The only way to avoid having the government, or a mob, seize and redistribute our stuff is to do it ourselves, freely, generously, and soon.

The sharing of goods in Jerusalem was not mandatory, not absolute, and not universal among believers. It was not "communism," even with a small "c." And it was probably not practiced much outside of Judea. Paul never speaks of it in his letters to churches across the Roman empire, nor does

Acts mention it happening in the churches he, Barnabas, and Silas founded. But the call of Christ to generosity to those in need was also heard in these places. It mostly took the form of hospitality (Rom. 12:13; Heb. 13:2) and sacrificial giving (Acts 11:27–30; Gal. 6:7–10; 2 Cor. 8:1–9:15; Titus 3:14). Same principles, different application: the gospel must be lived out by generous sharing of earthly goods, in order to meet urgent human needs.

Over time, the church came to be known for its care of the poor, both inside and outside of the church (see Gal. 6:10). In the fourth century, the frustrated emperor Julian "the Apostate" wrote to the pagan priest Arsacius: "It is disgraceful that, when . . . the impious [Christians] support not only their own poor but ours as well, all men see that our people lack aid from us." The ancient church, known for holiness of life, peaceableness, readiness to suffer for Christ, and generosity even toward their enemies, was unstoppable.

The prophetic ministry of Jesus, warning of God's coming judgment first on Judea and then the world, became the church's prophetic ministry. That prophetic ministry continues today, as we warn *our own* families, cities, nations, cultures of God's coming judgment, and live as a counterculture among and around them, pointing them always to the free offer of salvation: "Save yourselves from this crooked generation!" (Acts 2:40).

WHO IS THE SABBATH FOR?

The *Westminster Larger Catechism* notes that "the charge of keeping the Sabbath [is] more specially directed to governors of families and other superiors." It is for everyone, but *especially* for those with some degree of power and influence in the world. Business owners, for instance, have a duty to protect their people from overwork. Otherwise work (a gift from God, frustrating as it can be) becomes oppression. When we have authority and power over others (family members, employees, etc.) we are called to exercise a healthy "paternalism," helping our people make wise choices as parents help train their children (providing benefits like health insurance or a retirement contribution is another kind of paternalism). There are limits to this, depending on the relationship. But if those with authority and power don't encourage others to make good choices, they will encourage them to make bad choices. Help your people keep the Sabbath, so that your office or factory or home does not become an outpost of Egypt.

This may mean limiting your ambitions for wealth, self, and family. Isaiah cries, "Woe to those who join house to house, who add field to field, until there is no more room, and you are made to dwell alone in the midst of the land" (Isa. 5:8). This wasn't a warning against home renovations but against personal empire-building. Houses and fields were places of business and productivity. For these rich, plenty wasn't enough. They waited until their neighbors were deep in debt or otherwise distressed, and they bought the place next door at a fire-sale price. They built bigger barns while others cried "Uncle!" Later Isaiah warns against "doing your pleasure on my holy day" and tells his hearers to "call the Sabbath a delight" (Isa. 58:13). Does this mean "don't do anything you enjoy"? Of course not. "Your pleasure" is explained earlier in the chapter. They fast and humble themselves, but only as a cover for quarreling and fighting (Isa. 58:4). The same things that make people "join house to house" make them "do their own pleasure" on the Sabbath: greed, aggression, pride, ambition.

The alternative to empire-building and Sabbath breaking is to "pour yourself out for the hungry and satisfy the desire of the afflicted" (Isa. 58:10). If you do this, not only will you and your family be just fine, but God will use you for something far more glorious: the restoration and renewal of your community and your nation. "Your ancient ruins shall be rebuilt; you shall raise up the foundations of many generations; you shall be called the repairer of the breach, the restorer of streets to dwell in" (v. 12). Even better, if you call the Sabbath a delight, then "you shall take delight in the Lord" (v. 13). God promises to those who choose to walk in his ways both a lasting legacy and a restored bond with himself.

SABBATH MERCY FOR THE REST OF US

The call to let those who work for us rest is especially important for rulers, employers, managers, and business owners. But most of us don't make laws or run businesses. What about the rest of us, sometimes called "consumers" (wretched word)? All of us can abstain from unnecessary trade on the Lord's Day. Our "male servant and female servant" (Deut. 5:14) have a right to rest as we do. This means, at the most basic level, that unless it's necessary, we don't shop on Sunday—not coffee, not groceries, not gas, not online. (Just because you don't interact with someone at Amazon doesn't mean that they're not pulling and packing your order.) Extend rest to those who wait tables and pump gas.

The other person often ignored in Sabbath discussions is "the sojourner who is within your gates." This could be a very direct application: maybe you have non-citizen employees or contractors. The babysitter needs time off and so do the landscaping guys. You may also need to look further away. Most of us wear clothing and buy other products made in other lands, something very rare in biblical times when clothes were handmade, expensive, and styles varied from place to place. What kind of labor do we create for those who are far off, yet within the "gates" of our daily lives?

I can think of two reasons to give rest to those who aren't "our" people. One is backward-looking: "You shall remember that you were a slave in the land of Egypt" (Deut. 5:15). Elsewhere in the Law God brings up the same principle: "You shall not oppress the sojourner. You know the heart of a sojourner, for you were sojourners in the land of Egypt" (Exod. 23:9). You know what this life is like. Do not make it worse than it has to be. The other is forward-looking. In the New Covenant, the sojourner (a second-class resident in ancient Israel) *will be one of your people.* The gospel makes us all fellow citizens of the kingdom of God. Treat him as a brother, because he may well become your brother. This applies to all Christians in all lands today. We extend the kindness of the Sabbath to non-Christians and non-citizens of our countries because God did the same for us in Christ. We look forward to "every tongue confessing" Christ alongside in worship (Phil. 2:11). Show them mercy, invite them to the kingdom, and let them rest.

The people addressed first and foremost in the commandment are parents: "you or your son or your daughter." If you are a father or mother, you must set expectations and boundaries for your children. You must be "the decider" while your children are still under your roof. They might not like your restrictions, but it's still your job to do the restricting. Later they will be out of your hands, but for now they are your responsibility.

In our society children don't do much "work"—we have child labor laws, after all, and few of us live on farms. But actually, we expect them to do a lot of work. Homework is work and threatens to consume life for many school-age children. Set down a principle that your family doesn't do homework on the Lord's Day and stick with it. The kids may try to find their way around this. Maybe because they are undisciplined; maybe because they are overachievers and don't like to stop working; maybe because they are driven by *your* expectations. "Better is a little with the fear of the Lord than great treasure and trouble with it" (Prov. 15:16). Better a 2.5 GPA with the fear of the Lord than a 4.0 and be robbed of, or ignore, his day of rest.

There is another kind of work that many of our children perform, a kind we almost never think of as work. Play is natural, good, God-honoring, and essential to a healthy childhood. But since the 1800s, youth sports have become an *industry* worth about $19 billion in the United States, according to *USA Today*. Why do we let (or make) our kids do this? There are good reasons: sports can be fun, build skills and camaraderie, foster healthy competitiveness, and of course help the young become strong and athletic. But there are less-good reasons too. It lets parents live out their own dreams through their kids. Often parents and kids are nurturing dreams of professional sports or scholarships: this highlights that competitive sports *are work*. So while play is good, competitive sports should be off the table for Sundays. Might that destroy

Junior's pro soccer career before it starts? Yes, and that would be okay.

WELCOME TO THE FEAST

By now feasting on the Lord's Day is familiar. But there's a dimension of feasting that we haven't explored much: hospitality, or welcoming others to our feasts (and our homes and lives, in general).

In the Bible we see hospitality develop over time. In Genesis we have the powerful examples of Abraham and Lot (Gen. 18–19). A man of great dignity and wealth, Abraham fell over himself to prepare food and welcome three strangers when they appeared at his tent in the heat of midday. And although we often think of Lot as a bad guy, living as he did in the immoral city of Sodom, he actually stands out as an example when he welcomes two angels and attempts to protect them from assault at all costs. The Bible describes him as "righteous Lot" for this reason (2 Peter 2:7–8). Both of these men showed the proper attitude toward strangers: *philoxenia*, love of the stranger, the opposite of xenophobia, fear or hatred of the stranger. Home—whether house or tent or village or country—is safe. Being away from home is a position of danger and vulnerability (Prov. 27:8). It is honorable, as well as somewhat risky and often expensive, to welcome the stranger into your home.

Mercy in the Old Testament often took the form of hospitality, though not always. In some cases, such as the feasts of Esther and Nehemiah, each household was to feast and also to "send portions" to the needy. The bread that God mercifully provided in the desert had to be found and gathered by each family. But the bread that Jesus offers is himself: the ultimate hospitality, a welcome that costs the host his very life: "The bread that I will give for the life of the world is my flesh" (John 6:51).

Hospitality does not keep the needy at arm's length, like feeding the homeless at a soup kitchen. Instead, it shares with others the things that we love and enjoy. It doesn't just build community: it *is* community, *koinōnia*, having-in-common. Although other kinds of mercy are important as well, hospitality is normal and vital to the Christian life. It is Christians refusing to be *idiōtai*.

Hospitality is a witness to the kingdom of God and Christ. Jesus's works didn't just "prove" that his teaching was true: they *displayed* the kingdom. The kingdom of God is a place where the outsider is brought in, the sick are healed, the hungry are fed, so Jesus restored those alienated by their diseases and demons, gave sight to the blind, and fed multitudes. In the same way, the works of Christians make the gospel understandable to the world. We preach the Christ who "came not to be served but to serve, and to give his life as a ransom for many" (Matt. 20:28). Should we allow our

Sundays to be full of Martha-like busyness, or should we sit at the feet of Jesus and invite others to sit there with us?

Hospitality can be difficult. Things will go wrong. The nice family you invited to lunch will turn out to be weird. A kid will spill grape juice (pro tip: apple juice doesn't stain as badly). There will be mud. There might be awkward conversations. So what? We were dirty and stained and awkward, yet Christ welcomed us (Rom. 15:7). Strategize and make it work. If it's new, don't bite off too much at once: have people over once next month. Pray about it. Plan ahead, but be flexible. Think about a good mix of guests for conversation and comfort, and invite them ahead of time. Have one or two things you like to serve: there is no shame in serving soup, and you can make it on Saturday and warm it up. Make your house a place where people feel comfortable, not intimidated (or horrified). Clean up, but don't go crazy. Don't present a falsely perfect version of yourself and your family to impress others: just share the goodness God has shared with you. You are welcome at God's table. Welcome others to yours.

One thing about welcoming others on the Lord's Day (or any kind of mercy, for that matter): it can be tiring. Is this at odds with the call to rest? Yes and no. Hospitality, mercy of all kinds, and even simply making sure your family isn't worn out with the normal chores of the day: these can take a toll. But the mandate to rest must bow to holy work: "Or have you not read in the Law how on the Sabbath the priests in the temple profane the Sabbath and are guiltless?" (Matt. 12:5—more on this in Appendix 1). Be wise: know your limits. Remember that God will carry out his good work with or without you, and that while he does not need to rest, you do. Some Lord's Days you must make rest a priority even if it means delaying some of your mercy work. On others, you must labor a little harder than you would prefer for the sake of kindness and your testimony to the kingdom. On those days, count your missed nap, your bleary eyes, your all-talked-out tiredness as joy: the testing of your faith produces steadfastness (James 1:2).

MERCIFUL CHURCHES AND MERCIFUL PEOPLE

Mercy ministry is far too large a subject for a short chapter, but I want to distill a few principles of biblical kindness. First, the image of biblical mercy is of *sharing a meal:* this is "charity"—love—in the traditional sense. As we have opportunity, we should share our lives as well as our possessions. People have different capacities for this good work. You may be at a point in your life where other important demands mean you can do very little hospitality: that's fine. This is something to aspire to and work toward, not beat ourselves up over. Sometimes our mercy has to take a different form (sacrificial giving to meet pressing needs, for instance). If you can do nothing else, you can still pray.

Second, the program for mercy is *meeting pressing needs* (Titus 3:14). Not necessarily all of someone's felt needs. Not exactly their spiritual needs (though this will often go with meeting pressing needs), but the basics of human life: food, shelter, clothing, and medical care. We should pursue others having the same essentials that we want for ourselves. We probably should not literally give to everyone who asks, without some clear knowledge of their situation, or else we may be funding destructive habits. An ancient Jewish proverb, quoted in the Christian *Didache,* says, "Let your coin sweat in your hand, until you know to whom you should give it." My father, at the time a deacon, once had to deal with an angry church member who had received a lot of help and now felt that the church should fund a vacation in Florida! That was not a pressing need. We aim to see the basics met. Other help can be good, but it is icing on the cake.

Mercy should be *accompanied by prayer and the word of God*, whenever possible. We help others, even in small ways, in the name of Christ (Matt. 10:42). We are Christians, and Christ should get glory for our good works. For this reason I don't like the meme-ethics of "paying it forward" or "choosing kindness." Show mercy in the name of Jesus.

Helpful mercy *aims at getting those who are able to work, working* (2 Thess. 3:10; Eph. 4:28), *and those who can't work, praying* (1 Tim. 5:9–14). Idleness does not glorify the Lord of the Sabbath. We are made for work and rest. In a complex society, helping people work can take many forms. Some are simple: a contractor hires a low-skilled, unemployed guy to sweep up at the job site. A church helps a woman polish her interview skills and get professional-looking clothes and a haircut as she applies for jobs. Some are much more complex. The public schools in many areas are failing to give students either a good education or skills to earn a living. Alternative schools and apprenticeship programs may need to be built from the ground up. (John Calvin oversaw the founding of the Genevan Academy to meet the needs of a flood of refugees into sixteenth-century Switzerland—including their young people's need for vocational training.) But in every case, we should be aiming for good employment for all, either hands working or (for the elderly and sick) mouths praying.

Finally, biblical mercy *works for equality, not revolution*. The poor do not hold moral high ground against the rich and middle class. One of the lies of Marxism is that a revolution will put the virtuous "workers" in charge, and that they will rule with kindness and fairness for all, unlike the wicked capitalists.

Certainly, there are virtuous poor and wicked rich. There are also wicked poor and virtuous rich. Our goal in mercy is not to turn the tables, impoverishing the rich and enriching the poor. It is *fairness*.

Paul writes to the church in Corinth, leaning on them (pretty hard) to follow through on a contribution for famine-stricken Christians in Jerusalem: "I do not mean that others should be eased and you burdened, but that as a matter of fairness your abundance at the present time should supply their need, so that their abundance may supply your need, that there may be fairness" (2 Cor. 8:13–14). He ends, strikingly, by quoting from Exodus 16:18, a passage that originally spoke of Israel gathering manna: "As it is written, 'Whoever gathered much had nothing left over, and whoever gathered little had no lack'" (2 Cor. 8:15).

Everyone gets enough. Those who have more than they need don't cling to all of it. We are not to love the world's goods but to use them to love others. "If anyone has the world's goods and sees his brother in need, yet closes his heart against him, how does the love of God abide in him?" (1 John 3:17; see also Luke 12:15; Exod. 20:17).

MERCY IN WORSHIP

Mercy is an act of worship. This is part of why we give "tithes and offerings," "alms," and sometimes "freewill offerings" in worship. Paul told the church in Corinth to set aside their aid contributions "on the first day of every week" (1 Cor. 16:2), that is, at their worship services. Hebrews teaches that giving is just as much an act of worship as singing praise: "Through him then let us continually offer up a sacrifice of praise to God, that is, the fruit of lips that acknowledge his name. Do not neglect to do good and to share what you have, for such sacrifices are pleasing to God" (Heb. 13:15–16).

Showing mercy to others is a sacrifice that points us back to the sacrifice Christ made for us and for the life of the world (John 6:51). We give money, time, food, company: he gave everything. We welcome friends, family, fellow Christians, and sometimes strangers: he invites the unlovely of the whole world (including us). We have been shown mercy that we did not expect, do not deserve, and cannot repay.

Make your life a life of mercy. Start on the Sabbath.

10
EBENEZER

I WAS REFORMED BEFORE it was cool.

I grew up in a Reformed Presbyterian (RP) church plant in a college town in upstate New York. It was nearly an hour's drive to the nearest Reformed church (also RP). We were early homeschoolers: I started in sixth grade, and one of my best friends had been at the center of the lawsuit that led to homeschooling being legalized in my county.

These were the glorious days before the internet. As a homeschooled teen, I liked to listen to Rush Limbaugh in the afternoon when I should have been studying (having listened to National Public Radio for part of the morning). Magazines were a big part of life. While still in high school I read a ridiculous mix of periodicals: *The American Spectator,*

National Review, Books & Culture: A Christian Review, The New York Times Magazine, Guns & Ammo, and *American Rifleman* topped the list. The room we called "the library" held my parents' collection of theological, survivalist, and do-it-yourself books. Back issues of *Mother Earth News* shared a shelf with the short-lived *Journal of Christian Reconstruction.* Mom sewed clothes, and Dad kept bees.

Evangelicals in the 1980s and '90s were more proactive than they had been in the panicked, Hal Lindsey–influenced '70s. Instead of giving up on the "Late Great Planet Earth" or retreating into intentional communities that usually fizzled or turned into cults, Bible-believing Christians were more and more interested in bringing their faith to bear on the world. They didn't want to be on the defensive anymore. The writings of theonomists such as Rousas Rushdoony, Gary North, and David Chilton were audacious in their tone and their depth, which was a big breath of fresh air in comparison to the stagnation of the mainline churches and the end-times panic of the fundamentalists. Francis Schaefer's film series *How Shall We Then Live* was showing on VHS at many local churches. Douglas Wilson was starting to publish *Credenda/Agenda* in Moscow, Idaho. Solzhenitsyn was in Vermont. And long before the Babylon Bee, *The Wittenburg Door* was lampooning the daffier fringes of American Christianity.

Why the walk down memory lane? It's not just nostalgia. The late twentieth century was a kind of turning point for Christianity in America (and perhaps the world in general). Christianity was ceasing to be widely respected. The liberal theology of the big Protestant denominations was losing whatever public respect it had had. It was becoming clear that the relationship between church and world would be different from then on.

So thoughtful believers were asking big questions. How can we create (or recover) a distinctly Christian culture? How can we protect and stabilize the Christian communities we have? How can we actively extend the kingdom of God in a hostile world? These were the projects and pursuits of the time aimed at answering these questions: Christian education in various forms; parachurch organizations such as Focus on the Family; legal nonprofits such as the Rutherford Institute; abortion activism (an important meeting place for Evangelicals and Catholics); political activism by organizations such as the Moral Majority and later the Christian Coalition. There were also moments of overt rebellion (such as Waco and Ruby Ridge), which always ended with the rebels in jail or dead after a firefight.

With minor differences, the same questions were being asked by Jews in Galilee and Judea in the first century AD and by Jewish exiles in Babylon in the sixth century BC. They are also being asked today. The shelves of my office hold titles such as *A Secular Age* by Charles Taylor and *The Desire of the Nations: Rediscovering the Roots of Political Theology* by Oliver O'Donovan. Some explore the history of the faith interacting with the world. Others are more theological. Still others (*Going Public: Your Child Can Thrive In Public School* by the Pritchards; *The Tech-Wise Family* by Andy Crouch) are practical and tactical.

These are massively important questions, and we are not allowed to make up answers out of thin air or consult only human wisdom. We look to the Bible. I suggest we start here: *Without any expectation that the world will follow us, we will stubbornly practice a lifestyle of biblical obedience.*

That will include keeping the annoying, uncool, out-of-date Christian Sabbath. We must be willing to obey God in ways that are difficult and uncomfortable *for us*, not calling the world to bear burdens that we won't accept ourselves (Luke 11:46). And we let our private faith become public, intruding into work and school and social life, as much as it needs to. A purely private discipleship is no threat to the satanic powers at work in the world (Eph. 6:12).

THE SABBATH UNDERMINES "THE SYSTEM"

Culture and civilization are good things. Our first parents were told to "multiply and fill the earth and subdue it" (Gen. 1:28). Genesis and Exodus trace Abraham's descendants as they move from being nomadic herders of sheep and goats to farmers with houses and property. This movement sets the stage for cities and increasingly powerful, complicated societies. But culture and civilization always have the potential to turn into arrogance and rebellion against God. Babel is the first great example of this in Scripture, but it plays out in every age. The story of rise, decline, and fall is perpetual: it plays out in families, nations, empires, corporations, and churches. It will happen to us: maybe it is already happening.

"The system," which some rail against and some joke about, is real. (In his recent book *The Life We're Looking For*, Andy Crouch suggests we use the term Jesus did: mammon.) It's not a clever international plot, but an increasingly proud, powerful, oppressive tangle of human institutions and values. No one person, party, brand, or nation *is* the system, but there is a system, and it is a spiritual reality: "rulers and authorities in the heavenly places" (Eph. 3:10). Our warfare against it is spiritual, not physical.

As a priestly people, we must act on behalf of our civilization by humbling ourselves before God. The West, the modern world, the English-speaking world, and America cannot save themselves. No one can. The world needs the church to be what Jesus was—and what, through our union with Jesus, the church already is—a "sign that is opposed" (Luke 2:34), a "stone of stumbling, and a rock of offense" (Rom. 9:33). The transition from the realm of darkness to the kingdom of Christ is abrupt and rough, not easy and smooth (Col. 1:13). When we pretend that faith can be easy and smooth, that God can be our copilot and Christ a shoulder to cry on as we pursue our own agendas and preferences, we set ourselves up for a fall, and we lie to the world. The lost do not need easy: easy got them where they are. Only when they see Christians taking up their crosses and following Christ when it is hard will they believe that we mean what we say.

Samuel was both a prophet of God and the last great judge and leader of Israel before the time of the kings. After a time of disastrous defeats in battle with their enemies the Philistines, Samuel gathered the nation of Israel together at Mizpah to fast and repent before God of their idolatry.

The Philistines saw an opportunity and gathered their armies to attack the assembly at Mizpah. The people told Samuel to keep praying. This he did, as well as offering up a lamb sacrifice. "As Samuel was offering up the burnt offering, the Philistines drew near to attack Israel. But the Lord thundered with a mighty sound that day against the Philistines and threw them into confusion, and they were defeated before Israel" (1 Sam. 7:10).

As a memorial to this victory, Samuel raised up a standing stone and called it Ebenezer ("stone of help"). This was the beginning of a long period of safety and victory for Israel: "The hand of the Lord was against the Philistines all the days of Samuel. The cities that the Philistines had taken from Israel were restored to Israel, from Ekron to Gath, and Israel delivered their territory from the hand of the Philistines" (vv. 13–14).

Some of God's commandments are easy to understand: you can't have people murdering or stealing from each other, after all. Others seem irrational, standing like a rough stone, upright in the low hills of western Israel. The commandments have reasons, they have uses, but these are secondary to their primary purpose, which is *testimony*. The Sabbath is our Ebenezer: a hard-edged, rugged testimony to the fact that salvation is of the Lord. One day a week we lay aside our tools, wash off the sweat, stop pursuing our agendas, and feast and sing in honor of God. The living God is the source of every blessing. Not business, not family wealth, not the government, not our own hard work, not good luck, not our cleverness, not Manifest Destiny, and not heroic sacrifice. *God.*

The Sabbath is an act of dissent from the world of Egypt, the world of total work. On it we declare that everything good we have is a gift. It doesn't matter whose name is on the deed to the house or the farm: "The earth is the Lord's and the fullness thereof" (Ps. 24:1). Though our earthly masters may think they own us, we will one day judge them and angels (1 Cor. 6:1–3).

The Sabbath is a step toward changing what is wrong in our world. A society that never rests is capable of great things, especially of creating great wealth, but with great wealth comes great inequality. Inequality doesn't seem like a problem if you're doing well. But it's a powder keg, an accident waiting to happen. The Sabbath stops the rich and poor alike and tells them to be still before the God of all the earth. It's an expression of brotherhood for our fellow Christians, especially the poor. And it's an invitation to the whole world to become our brothers, share our rest.

The Sabbath is not just an act of protest or dissent, but an act of repentance and humility for us as Christians. "For it is time for judgment to begin with the household of God" (1 Peter 4:17 NASB). Whether we like it or not, our obedience to God is a judgment on the world. But we are judged as well as judging. We may not tell the world that it has a problem without taking the logs out of our own eyes. This is an unusual kind of repentance, because it isn't expressed with sackcloth, ashes, tears, and fasting. Like the older brother in the parable of the prodigal son, Sabbath repentance means setting aside our disappointment and resentment and going inside to the party the Father is throwing (Luke 15:11–32).

In many countries, a religious day of rest is protected by law. The Sabbath means that we live with patience and with dignity (1 Tim. 2:2), not claiming victim status, but using our legal rights for the sake of the gospel and obedience to God, as Paul did in Philippi (Acts 16:37). We are not seeking to conquer the nations, by ballots or bullets. That is the Lord's prerogative. He has done it before, and he will do it again. How many times do the psalms tell us to wait for the Lord? "Be still before the Lord and wait patiently for him; fret not yourself over the one who prospers in his way, over the man who carries out evil devices!" (Ps. 37:7). A church that patiently obeys shows the world what the world could be, and what it one day will be, when every knee bows and every tongue confesses that Jesus is Lord (Phil. 2:9–11).

How does change come about in the world? From society, bubbling up into government? Or from government reaching out and down to reshape society? Probably a bit of both, but it doesn't matter. When the church takes the Kingdom seriously—seriously enough to suffer for its obedience—the world pays attention, and when the world pays attention, it changes. Therefore our discipleship must be visible. We must keep our holy day as we are able, whether or not those around us respect us for doing so, whether or not it hurts our business profits, whether or not it's convenient.

My strategy in this book has been to look at the Sabbath from every angle I can think of, in hope of convincing you to rest and give others rest on the first day of the week. This is a controversial discussion, and I know that I will have gone too far for some and not far enough for others. I have not focused on deep-dive interpretations ("exegesis") of particular passages, and there is a reason for that. Exegesis is much more difficult and rare than people (including pastors) think. Like statistics, exegesis often gets used to support what people already believe. Some books about the Sabbath get so far "down in the weeds" that they fall into this trap. Instead I have presented what *I* find convincing. In defending any idea, that's the only honest thing an author can do.

Now you must weigh what you have read and decide. Does the evidence point where I think it points? To a continuation of the weekly Sabbath for Christians, as a day of worship first and foremost, then feasting, rest, and mercy? Does the fourth commandment call Christians to rest (in this full sense) and share that rest with others?

Proverbs makes a promise: "Honor the Lord with your wealth and with the firstfruits of all your produce; then your barns will be filled with plenty, and your vats will be bursting with wine" (Prov. 3:9–10). When we keep the Sabbath, we give to God the firstfruits of our *time*. Keep his holy day and see what he does: for you, for your family, for his church, and for the nations who (whether we realize it or not) are watching us closely, to see if we really are any different.

APPENDIX 1:
PASTORS AND SABBATICALS

IF YOU'RE NOT FAMILIAR with the term, "sabbatical" is short for "sabbatical year" or "sabbatical leave," and it means an extended period of time away from one's normal work for travel, research, writing, or rest. The idea has Old Testament roots—remember the "sabbath years" (Exod. 23; Lev. 23, 25)? But this is not a strict, straightforward application of those passages. As far as I can tell, the idea was picked up by professors at Harvard University in the late 1800s and has spread through academia and sometimes into the worlds of business and the church.

I am going to make a case that pastors need sabbaticals. This may seem a little selfish of an author who is a pastor, but I am not trying to convince my own congregation (who are already convinced and granted me one when I needed it badly).

PASTORAL PRESSURE AND BURNOUT

The work pressures pastors are under are not totally unique, but they are unusual. Pastors are under scrutiny like politicians, but without the public respect and clout that draw many into politics. They are "always on," often working seven days a week, much like farmers or entrepreneurs, but without the potential for profit that business can bring and without the multigenerational payoff that farmers expect (the work that pastors do hopefully lasts for eternity—but a pastor cannot retire and hand over his pulpit to his children).

In the past the work of pastoring was somewhat seasonal and often light. Low salaries were normal, but that was somewhat made up for by flexible time, a church-owned house, and sometimes a plot of land to farm (like the Levites of old). In his journal, Josiah Dodds, the founding pastor of a Reformed Presbyterian church in Kansas, marked many days in July 1867 as "Plowed and hoed potatoes" or "Weeding potatoes" or "Writing—studying." The expectations of most churches were straightforward: Preach to us; baptize, marry, and bury us. Along with the ruling elders, visit us from time to time, and be there in times of crisis. Some pastors put in very long hours; some didn't.

Some churches still own a parsonage or manse, which is great. But the ministers' farms are gone, and the time is much less flexible. The twentieth century brought new expectations. Pastors must be counselors. They must administer a raft of responsibilities that they may or may not have talent for. They must care for geographically scattered congregations, spending hours in the car on visits. They must always be reachable by phone. The internet age, and especially the smartphone and social media, has supercharged all of this. Technology must be mastered and kept up with. Preaching is constantly compared with that of great (and not-so-great) celebrity pastors. Some churches expect a social media presence—but whether or not it's expected, far too many pastors are distracted by the internet, and wind up burning time and the linings of their stomachs fighting for truth on Facebook or Twitter.

Whatever the reasons—changing expectations, internet pressures, lack of personal discipline, a generational notion that work should always be fulfilling, etc.—I have seen a lot of pastors burn out or leave the pastorate wrecked (or dead). To be clear, that is not entirely within the control of a congregation, and men bear responsibility for their own actions and the ways they deal with pressure. On the other hand pastors are not just shepherds but sheep, and their well-being and longevity in service should be a concern to every church member.

Appendix 1: Pastors and Sabbaticals

MISSING SABBATHS

Leisure, claimed Josef Pieper in his famous book, is the basis of culture. Leisure in the ancient sense was not laziness or the consumption of entertainment. It was setting aside work to rest, feast, talk, and think. Aristotle said, "We work that we may have leisure." One of the themes of this book is that Sabbath, God-ordained leisure, is the goal or point of work. No matter how important or successful our work is, if we cannot step back and enjoy it, we are missing out on some of God's blessing.

Pieper also noted leisure and festivals go together and worship is at the heart of both. Most certainly, that is true of the Lord's Day. The central duty of worship turns the day into a day of rest, feasting, and mercy. But someone must host the feast and lead the service of worship. That burden falls heaviest on pastors. Remember what Jesus said about the priests? "Have you not read in the Law how on the Sabbath the priests in the temple profane the Sabbath and are guiltless?" (Matt. 12:5). In a sense, pastors forgo Sabbath rest week after week, year after year, so that others can have it.

Many make up for this by taking a "pastor's Monday" or another day of the week off. In his book *Working the Angles,* author and Presbyterian pastor Eugene Peterson described his "Sabbath" in great detail. On Mondays he and his wife would quietly pack sandwiches and head out of town for an all-day hike, breaking silence only for prayer and a meal together. In the evening they would read or "putter around the house." This sounds like a good day off, but it isn't the Sabbath. The day of the week is nonnegotiable: the Christian Sabbath happens on the day of the Lord's resurrection. Further, Sabbath is not just something *I* do (as an individual), or even a day for family togetherness (I once heard a pastor refer to Sunday as "Family Day"—yikes!): it's a day for the church to gather in honor of the risen and reigning Lord. Monday through Saturday can be days off, but they cannot be the Sabbath.

That means that, for good reasons, unavoidably, pastors miss out on the Sabbath leisure that others enjoy. And that's a problem.

SABBATH NOW OR SABBATH LATER

Nothing can be done to get *those* Sabbaths back, and most pastors wouldn't trade their jobs for another. But there is a price to be paid for the always-on, no-Sundays-off life.

Sabbath years are mentioned not only in the laws that command them, but in Old Testament warnings of judgment. In Leviticus, God warns that idolatry and rebellion will be punished with exile from the Promised Land: "Then the land shall enjoy its Sabbaths as long as it lies desolate, while you are in your enemies' land; then the land shall rest, and enjoy its Sabbaths. As long as it lies desolate it shall

Appendix 1: Pastors and Sabbaticals

have rest, the rest that it did not have on your Sabbaths when you were dwelling in it" (Lev. 26:34–35). At the end of 2 Chronicles, after a chilling description of Jerusalem's fall to the armies of Babylon, the author adds this postscript:

> He took into exile in Babylon those who had escaped from the sword, and they became servants to him and to his sons until the establishment of the kingdom of Persia, to fulfill the word of the LORD by the mouth of Jeremiah, until the land had enjoyed its Sabbaths. All the days that it lay desolate it kept Sabbath, to fulfill seventy years. (2 Chron. 36:20–21)

Because Judah didn't give the land the Sabbaths God had ordained, God would give the land its Sabbaths despite them. Whether or not they are in knowing rebellion, God will do the same to people who do not observe his Sabbaths. Sabbath now or Sabbath later.

My point here is not to condemn anyone: for the most part, pastors are trying to be humble, conscientious servants, and congregations are trying to take good care of them. My point is that it is wise and right to recognize that pastors accrue a "Sabbath debt" over years of service, and it is wise and right to try to help them pay down that debt. Otherwise, we should expect it to catch up with them, and should not be surprised when we see breakdowns in health and morale, errors in judgment, and careers cut short.

HOW TO GIVE YOUR PASTOR A SABBATICAL

For the sake of longevity and health in the ministry, it is good for churches to give their pastors sabbaticals. Whenever possible, this should be part of the terms of a call. But there are details to figure out.

What should a pastor do on his sabbatical? This depends on his needs, energy level, and the length of the sabbatical. It's hard to tackle a significant writing project, for instance, in less than six months. A classic use of sabbatical time is research. Another is travel, sometimes to Israel or another region important to church history or the study of the Bible. But I would recommend calling time off to do research and writing something like "study leave," not sabbatical. And it is a rare pastor who has the means to travel the world for 3–12 months.

Many pastors drag themselves into their leave, barely keeping it together, and rest is the only thing they should do, especially if it is three months long or less. You will need to work with your pastor to figure out what he needs. Be aware that he will probably be reluctant to recognize or admit his need of a rest. You're more likely to get an accurate picture if you talk to his wife!

Is sabbatical vacation? That depends. Vacations were perhaps less important when work was generally "slow and steady"

Appendix 1: Pastors and Sabbaticals

(not just for pastors but for farmers and a host of other occupations). But when work is "fast and unrelenting," vacation is a necessity. Maybe it is my Italian blood talking, but American workers work too much. Work is good, but only when punctuated by rest (you've read the book so I won't repeat myself). Depending on the term of the sabbatical, and how often sabbatical is taken, it might replace or be added to vacation time. Friends who have taken one- or two-months sabbaticals usually have them tacked onto their vacation (for a total of two to three months off that year). Other friends have had six-month sabbaticals and haven't taken a seventh month off.

How does pay work? The classic academic sabbatical involved a professor traveling elsewhere, usually on a grant, to do research and writing for an entire year. He or she would probably be on reduced pay from the home university. Most pastors are paid full-time through their sabbatical, although I can imagine a sabbatical in which a pastor takes up different paid work and his church salary is reduced accordingly.

Who preaches and does pastoral care? Obviously if a church has more than one pastor, a sabbatical is a time for the others to step up to the plate. However, most of my time in ministry has been as a solo pastor, and most churches in my denomination are as well. In Presbyterian churches, ruling elders are allowed to preach, and most ruling elders should do so occasionally (sabbatical or no). This is also a great opportunity to bring in seminary students, retired preachers, pastors from nearby (theologically sound) churches. Pastoral care is the work of all elders, and the ones who are not on leave should plan to carry out visitation and member care that the pastor normally would. With that said, the session might decide that some non-emergency visitation and care (as well as nonessential teaching) can take a hiatus.

How often, and how long? This one is tough. It should not be so often or long that the congregation is financially crippled or the bond between pastor and church is weakened. But it must be often enough, and long enough. Below are three sample policies, from different churches:

CHURCH A (one pastor)	• Starting in year 4, pastor is allowed 3 weeks sabbatical (as well as vacation). Additional 3 weeks accrue every year after that. (Year 4, 3 weeks; year 5, 6 weeks; year 6, 9 weeks; etc.)
	• In year 7, if he hasn't taken one, the session will lean on him to do so.
	• Sabbaticals are for rest.
CHURCH B (multiple pastors)	• Every other year, each pastor gets a 1-month sabbatical (as well as vacation).
	• On the third cycle (year 6, 12, etc.), he gets a 2-month sabbatical.
	• Pastors cannot take sabbaticals in the same year.
	• Sabbaticals are for rest.

Appendix I: Pastors and Sabbaticals

CHURCH C
(multiple pastors)
- Every 3 years, each pastor gets a 3-month sabbatical (as well as vacation).
- Pastors cannot take sabbaticals in the same year.
- Sabbaticals are for rest.

OTHER OFFICERS, TOO

What I have said about pastors applies to other church officers, too. Conscientious elders and deacons can get burnt out on their ministry work—and they are nearly always unpaid and often serving on top of their day jobs. I suggest a policy of regular time off for the officers: perhaps a year off out of every seven. In a small church this may be a good spur toward scheduling elder or deacon elections and not getting used to the veterans carrying all the weight.

THINK ABOUT IT

Pastors benefit greatly from extended breaks from their regular work. Pastoring is a strange brew of a job, requiring people skills; "area expertise" in theology, history, the Bible, and biblical languages; administrative acumen (sadly lacking in me); vision and imagination; attention to detail; and initiative. Any kind of leader benefits from times of leisure, tastes of the "contemplative life." US Army Col. David Hackworth wrote in *About Face*, "Be a doer and a self-starter—aggressiveness and initiative are two most admired qualities in a leader—*but you must also put your feet up and think*" (emphasis added).

Giving your pastor a sabbatical may seem like a luxury (I have heard it described as something only rich big city churches do!), but it seems increasingly like a necessity. Start planning a sabbatical for your pastor *now*. Even knowing that a real break is coming will be life-giving for him. He, like many other people, is tempted to find his identity and worth in his work. Let him know that you think of him not only as a professional but also as a beloved brother in Christ.

APPENDIX 2:
SAMPLE LETTERS TO EMPLOYERS

THE FIRST LETTER IS ADAPTED from one developed by Christ Church (Reformed Presbyterian) in Brownsville, Indiana. Pastors, elders, or others working with a church member who is being forced to work Sundays should feel free to use or adapt it as needed. Before doing so, be sure to meet with the member and discuss the teaching of the church on the Sabbath. If they are not clear in their own minds, a letter will not do much. Also discuss with them the need for a humble and winsome attitude when working with their employers on this issue. I suggest sending the letter *by hand*, at least initially.

If the employer will not give an answer, or is hostile, consider *adapting* the second letter, which has been copied (unchanged) from the website of a Seventh-day Adventist organization, and sending it by hand or by registered mail. Historically the Adventists are much better at sticking up for their belief in a day of rest than Reformed or Presbyterians are.

SAMPLE LETTER #1
[Church Letterhead]

[Employer
Address
City, State, Zip Code]

[Date]

Dear Employer:

Our church community understands that constitutional religious liberties in a diverse society present challenges for employers. That is why [name of church] wants to clearly state our sincerely held religious beliefs and request reasonable accommodation for the church member bearing this letter so that he or she may not be scheduled to work on Sundays.

We believe and instruct our members that God teaches us to love and obey Him by following the moral law summarized in the Ten Commandments. These include commandments not to murder and not to steal (the sixth and eighth commandments), as well as the fourth commandment which sets aside one day a week for worship and not for labor: "Remember the Sabbath day to keep it holy. Six days you shall labor and do all your work, but the seventh day is a Sabbath for the Lord your God" (Exodus 20:8–10). There are many religious, social, and health benefits that flow from adherence to this command.

Our official church documents, called the Westminster Standards, explain: "the fourth commandment requires the keeping holy one whole day in seven, to be a holy Sabbath"; and, "the Sabbath is to be sanctified by a holy resting all that day and in God's worship." We also believe that because Christ's resurrection occurred on the first day of the week (a Sunday), the Sabbath is to be observed on that day each week: "From the resurrection of Christ the day was changed to the first day of the week [Sunday], which in Scripture is called the Lord's Day, and is to be the Christian Sabbath."

Therefore, please consider reasonable accommodation so that the bearer of this letter can practice his or her religious conviction and rest and worship the whole day on Sunday. *We appreciate every effort you make to enable our church members to honor this doctrine of our faith.* We would also point out that, in addition to requiring rest on Sunday, the fourth commandment also requires diligent labor the rest of the week. We believe the bearer of this letter would gladly adjust their schedule on the other days of the week in order to accommodate this simple religious conviction.

Thank you for your consideration.
[name of pastor, elder, or other authority]
[name of church]

SAMPLE LETTER #2
[Date]

[Employer
Address
City, State, Zip Code]
RE: Accommodation for Religious Belief and Practice

Dear [HR Person's Name]:

I am writing this letter on behalf of your employee, [church member] who is a member of the [name of church]. [He/She] has requested a schedule that would accommodate [his/her] religious observance of the Sabbath. [Name of church denomination]'s observe the Sabbath, one of the Ten Commandments, from sundown Friday to sundown Saturday, and abstain from secular work during those hours. We will greatly appreciate your giving due consideration to [his/her] request for a scheduling accommodation so that [name] does not have to make the impossible choice between faithfulness to God and keeping her job.

In 2015, the Supreme Court clarified the requirements of Federal law, Title VII of the Civil Rights Act of 1964, 42 U.S.C. Section 2000e. The Supreme Court held that employers cannot make a worker's need for religious accommodation "a motivating factor" in an adverse employment action, such as termination. The Court explained that a company must do more than simply follow its religion neutral employment policies—it must make affirmative efforts to provide religious accommodation, even giving the employee who needs accommodation "favored treatment." The Supreme Court explained the law with the following example:

An employer may not make an applicant's religious practice, confirmed or otherwise, a factor in employment decisions. For example, suppose that an employer thinks (though he does not know for certain) that a job applicant may be an orthodox Jew who will observe the Sabbath, and thus be unable to work on Saturdays. If the applicant actually requires an accommodation of that religious practice, and the employer's desire to avoid the prospective accommodation is a motivating factor in his decision, the employer violates Title VII. See *EEOC v. Abercrombie & Fitch*, 135 S.Ct. 2028 (2015).

In the typical employment setting, there are various methods that may be utilized to provide scheduling accommodations. These include

- adjusting the employee's schedule;
- arranging shift swaps with other employees, either on a day-by-day basis, or for a period of time;
- permitting the employee to utilize paid leave, such as vacation or sick leave;
- permitting the employee to take unpaid leave; and
- refraining from assigning attendance points for absences on account of the religious observance.

Remember, Title VII places the obligation on the employer to provide religious accommodation, it does not permit the employer to delegate that responsibility to the employee.

In his concurring opinion, Justice Alito stressed the Court's holding that "neutral work rules" do not excuse a company's failure to accommodate a religious practice. Examples of such "neutral work rules" or policies include

- rotating or other scheduling practices;
- policies regarding swapping shifts;
- policies regarding the use of paid and unpaid leave;
- attendance policies; and
- discipline policies.

According to the Supreme Court, an employer cannot simply apply these sorts of "neutral work rules" if the end result is to discipline or terminate the employee who seeks religious accommodation.

I am confident that you will be able to arrange a suitable accommodation for [name], and that when you do so, you will secure [his/her] loyalty and dedication to be the best employee [he/she] can be. [His/Her] respect for God's authority that leads [him/her] to observe the Sabbath will also translate into respect for the best interests of your company, and giving [his/her] very best service at work.

Thank you in advance for your anticipated cooperation with this request.

Sincerely,
Pastor [name]

SOURCES

Augustine of Hippo. *The City of God Against the Pagans* 19.24. From *From Irenaeus to Grotius: A Sourcebook in Christian Political Thought*. O. O'Donovan & J. Lockwood O'Donovan, eds. Grand Rapids: Eerdmans, 1999.

Augustine of Hippo. "Contra Faustum, Book XIX." New Advent. Accessed October 5, 2022. https://www.newadvent.org/fathers/140619.htm

Bjork, Christopher, and William Hoynes. "Youth sports needs a reset. Child athletes are pushed to professionalize too early." *USA Today*. March 24, 2021. https://www.usatoday.com/story/opinion/voices/2021/03/24/youth-sports-competitive-covid-19-expensive-column/4797607001/

Blixen, Karen et al. 2013. *Babette's Feast.* [United States]: The Criterion Collection.

Brueggemann, Walter. *Sabbath As Resistance: Saying No to the Culture of Now.* Louisville: Westminster John Knox, 2017.

Carson, D.A., ed. *From Sabbath to Lord's Day: A Biblical, Historical and Theological Investigation.* Eugene: Wipf & Stock, 2000.

Chantry, Walter. *Call the Sabbath a Delight.* Carlisle, PA: Banner of Truth, 1991.

Crouch, Andy. *The Life We're Looking For: Reclaiming Relationship in a Technological World.* Colorado Springs: Convergent, 2022.

Dennison, James T. *The Market Day of the Soul: The Puritan Doctrine of the Sabbath in England, 1532–1700.* Morgan, PA: Soli Deo Gloria, 2001.

Dodds, Belle Torrence, to the Pastor, elders, and members of Winchester Reformed Presbyterian Church. Unpublished letter. August 16, 1898. From the archives of Winchester Reformed Presbyterian Church, Winchester, KS.

Edelheit, Aaron *The Hard Break: The Case for a 24/6 Lifestyle.* n.p.: Ideapress Publishing, 2018.

"The Epistle of Barnabas." *The Apostolic Fathers, Vol. I.* Translated by Kirsopp Lake. Loeb Classical Library 24. Cambridge, MA: Harvard University Press, 1985.

Ford, Tom. "Questlove: Why Cooking Is Harder Than Jazz." Mr. Porter, February 7, 2019. https://www.mrporter.

com/en-us/journal/the-interview/questlove-why-cooking-is-harder-than-jazz/4249?setupsession=false

Gaffin, Richard. *Calvin and the Sabbath: The Controversy of applying the Fourth Commandment.* Fearn, Ross-shire, Scotland: Christian Focus, 2009.

Hackworth, David. *About Face; the Odyssey of an American Warrior.* New York: Simon & Schuster, 1989.

Heschel, Abraham Joshua. *The Sabbath: Its Meaning for Modern Man.* New York: Farrar, Straus, and Giroux, 2005.

Hudson, Hugh, et al. 1981. *Chariots of Fire* [United States]. 20th Century Fox.

Julian Caesar. "To Arsacius, High-priest of Galatia." Letters of Julian/Letter 22. Wikisource. Accessed October 5, 2022. https://en.wikisource.org/wiki/Letters_of_Julian/Letter_22

Julian, Kate. "Why Are Young People Having So Little Sex?" *The Atlantic Monthly*, December 2018.

Kipling, Rudyard. "The Gods of the Copybook Headings." *Rudyard Kipling's Verse: Definitive Edition.* Garden City, NY: Doubleday & Co., 1940.

Kreglinger, Gisela. *The Spirituality of Wine.* Grand Rapids: Eerdmans, 2016.

Kreider, Alan. *The Patient Ferment of the Early Church: The Improbable Rise of Christianity in the Roman Empire.* Ada, MI: Baker Academic, 2016.

LeFebvre, Michael. *Liturgies of Creation: Understanding Calendars in Old Testament Context.* Downers Grove, IL: InterVarsity, 2019.

Mann, Charles. *1491: New Revelations of the Americas Before Columbus.* New York: Vintage, 2006.

"Mekilta on Exodus 31.13 (109*b*)." *New Testament Background: Selected Documents: Revised and Expanded Edition.* C.K. Barrett, ed. New York: HarperOne, 1995.

Moore, Joseph. *Founding Sins: How a Group of Antislavery Radicals Fought to Put Christ into the Constitution.* New York: Oxford University Press, 2015.

O'Dwyer, Philip. "The Irish and Substance Abuse." Health Research Board [of Ireland] National Drugs Library. https://www.drugsandalcohol.ie/4320/1/738-0695604.pdf

Paglia, Camille. *Sexual Personae: Art and Decadence from Nefertiti to Emily Dickinson.* New York: Random House, 1991.

Peterson, Eugene. *Working the Angles: The Shape of Pastoral Integrity.* Grand Rapids: Eerdmans, 1993.

Pieper, Josef. *Leisure: The Basis of Culture.* Translated by Alexander Dru. San Francisco: Ignatius, 2009.

Ravikant, Naval. (@NavalBot) 2018. "Tweet text" 4:26 p.m. https://twitter.com/navalbot/status/1070066832420163585?lang=en

"Request—pastor letter." Church State Council. Accessed June 2, 2022. http://www.churchstate.org/index.php?id=181

Scheidel, Walter. *The Great Leveler: Violence and the History of Inequality from the Stone Age to the Twenty-First Century*. Princeton: Princeton University Press, 2017.

Scott, Ridley. 2000. *Gladiator*. United States: DreamWorks Distribution

Suetonius. "Claudius, 25." *New Testament Background: Selected Documents: Revised and Expanded Edition*. C.K. Barrett, ed. New York: HarperOne, 1995.

"Synod of Laodicea (4th Century)." New Advent. Accessed October 5, 2022. https://www.newadvent.org/fathers/3806.htm

Taylor, Sydney. *The All of a Kind Family*. New York: Random House, 1979.

Tertullian. "Ad Nationes, Book I." New Advent. Accessed October 5, 2022. https://www.newadvent.org/fathers/03061.htm

Tertullian. "The Chaplet." New Advent. Accessed October 5, 2022. https://www.newadvent.org/fathers/0304.htm

[Untitled letter requesting Sabbath accommodation]. Christ Church of Brownsville, Indiana. Accessed June 14, 2016. http://ccrp.church/wp-content/uploads/2013/12/Sabbath-Letter.pdf

Vincent, Isabel, and Melissa Klein. "High wire strewn through city lets Jews keep the faith." *New York Post*. May 24, 2015. https://nypost.com/2015/05/24/high-wire-strewn-through-city-lets-jews-keep-the-faith/

Washington, George. "To the Hebrew Congregation in Newport, Rhode Island, August 18, 1790." *Writings*. Library of America 91. New York: Literary Classics of the United States, 1997.

Wilder, Laura Ingalls. *Farmer Boy*. New York and Evanston, IL: Harper & Row, 1953.

Wright, Nicholas T. *The New Testament and the People of God*. Minneapolis: Fortress Press, 1992.

FURTHER READING ON MERCY AND CHARITY

Butterfield, Rosaria. *The Gospel Comes With A House Key: Practicing Radically Ordinary Hospitality in Our Post-Christian World.* Wheaton, IL: Crossway, 2018.

Chester, Tim. *Good News to the Poor: Social Involvement and the Gospel.* Wheaton, IL: Crossway, 2013.

Corbett, Steve, and Brian Fikkert. *When Helping Hurts: How to Alleviate Poverty Without Hurting the Poor . . . and Yourself.* Chicago: Moody, 2014.

"The Didache, Or Teaching of the Twelve Apostles." *The Apostolic Fathers, Vol. I.* Translated by Kirsopp Lake. Loeb Classical Library 24. Cambridge, MA: Harvard University Press, 1985.

Ehlig, Billy, and Ruby K. Payne. *What Every Church Member Should Know About Poverty*. Highlands, TX: aha! Process, 1999.

Keller, Timothy. *Ministries of Mercy: The Call of the Jericho Road*. 2nd ed. Phillipsburg, NJ: P&R, 1997.

Lupton, Robert. *Toxic Charity: How Churches and Charities Hurt Those They Help (And How to Reverse It)*. New York: HarperOne, 2012.

Lupton, Robert. *Charity Detox: What Charity Would Look Like If We Cared About Results*. New York: HarperOne, 2016.

GRASSMARKET PRESS

GRASSMARKET PRESS is named for the square in Edinburgh where many Reformed Presbyterians (also known as Covenanters) were martyred for preaching Jesus Christ's reign over Scotland and all earth. Though many lost their lives, their witness for Christ endures. Grassmarket Press aims to help Christians know, practice, and stand for their faith.

THE BEDROCK SERIES aims to provide clear, concise books on Christian doctrine and life from a Reformed and Presbyterian perspective.